YOU MAKE THE DIFFERENCE

OTHER BOOKS BY ERIC BUTTERWORTH

Discover the Power Within You
How to Break the Ten Commandments
In the Flow of Life
Life Is for Living
Life Is for Loving
Spiritual Economics: The Prosperity Process
Unity of All Life

You Make the Difference

ERIC BUTTERWORTH

Harper & Row, Publishers, San Francisco

Cambridge, Hagerstown, New York, Philadelphia

1817   London, Mexico City, São Paulo, Singapore, Sydney

FIRST EDITION

Library of Congress Cataloging in Publication Data

Butterworth, Eric.
   YOU MAKE THE DIFFERENCE.

   1. Conduct of life. I. Title.
BJ1581.2.B85   1984   158'.1   76-9959
ISBN 0-06-061271-1

84 85 86 87 88 10 9 8 7 6 5 4 3 2 1

To Olga

*Whose tender, patient, and loving support
has made all the difference.*

Contents

Introduction   xi

I. The Importance of You

    1. The Need to Be Yourself   3
    2. The Great Frontier   4
    3. Playing the Role   6
    4. You Are Important!   8
    5. Happiness Is Homemade   9
    6. Action an Aid to Feeling   11
    7. Hidden Treasure   12
    8. What Are You Saying to Yourself?   14
    9. What Are You Seeing?   16
   10. This One Thing I Do   17
   11. The Woodcarver and the Bear   19

II. Thinking Makes It So

   12. Thinking About Thinking   23
   13. The World You Live In   24
   14. It's What's Inside That Counts   26
   15. How to Reverse Adversity   28
   16. The Right Angle   29
   17. The Power of Suggestion   31
   18. The Fine Art of Changing One's Mind   33
   19. Creative Imagination   34
   20. Can You Imagine That?   36
   21. How to Manage Your Emotions   38
   22. Keeping Up with Yesterday   40

III. Getting Along with People

   23. The One Creative Force   45
   24. How to Get Along with People   46

25. The Opportunity of Marriage 48
26. The Hunger for Appreciation 50
27. Be an Ordinary Person 51
28. The Art of Listening 53
29. How to Give and Receive Criticism 55
30. The Grace of Receiving 57
31. Praise 58

IV. **Living Healthfully**

32. The Key to Mental Health 63
33. Your Fountain of Youth 64
34. The Prince and the Statue 66
35. When the Heat's On 67
36. How to Avoid Middle-Age Letdown 69
37. How to Get Out of Your Shell 71
38. The Quest for Attractiveness 74
39. The Birthday of Your Life 75

V. **Work and Success**

40. Your Possible Dream 81
41. Making the Breaks of Life 83
42. The Lifters and the Leaners 84
43. The Master Plan! 86
44. A Cosmic View of Work 87
45. The Healing of the Economy 89
46. How to Find Employment 91
47. Giving Yourself Away 92
48. From Futility to Significance 94
49. The Feel of Success 96
50. Do You Have Soft Shoulders? 97
51. Your Work As a "Calling" 99

VI. **Standing Up to Life**

52. How to Make Decisions 103
53. Up-to-Par Insurance 105

54. Your Innate Power to Overcome 107
55. Handle Your Fears! 108
56. Stand Up to Life 110
57. People Who Live in the Wilderness 112
58. How to Meet Interruptions 114
59. Taking the Simple Way 115
60. Your Genius for Good Fortune 117
61. How to Get Rid of Your Crutches 119

VII. The Art of Letting Go

62. Meet Mr. Rushmore 123
63. Twenty-Four Hours to Live 124
64. A New Look at Tension 126
65. The Need for Silence 127
66. Relax and Let Go 129
67. You Need Never Be Tired 131
68. Sanctuary for You 132
69. Tranquility for You 134
70. Slow Down and Catch Up 136
71. The Art of Sleeping 138
72. Freedom and Solitude 140
73. From Fretting to Letting 141

Introduction

It is said that "hope springs eternal in the human breast"; but the dream of better things is sometimes reduced to a faded glimmer. And there are those who cry out with Shakespeare's Juliet: "Come weep with me; past hope, past cure, past help!"

Many persons, trapped in situations and relationships that become increasingly destructive and depleting, move from resistance to downright resignation. At this point we may often hear the cliché of submission: "What can I do? I have no choice."

I have counseled with thousands of people through the years. In trying to bring them some measure of help or comfort, or to ignite some spark that will lead to their transformation, I have always tried to reduce the concepts of metaphysics and philosophy to the least common denominator. And I have discovered that the one simple thought that is most revealing and helpful to the person in deep inner turmoil is this: *You always have a choice!* Five words that strike right at the heart of deep-seated feelings of hopelessness and despair. Again and again I have seen the spark of hope rekindled as I have said, "Take hope: there is still something you can do. There is no choiceless life. You always have a choice!"

You may be living in trying times, faced with a shaky economy that is beyond your control, but which is having a progressively detrimental effect on your personal security. You may see yourself as an innocent bystander in a world of "wars and rumors of war," in a society rife with inequities and injustices, and in a community stricken with blight and depravity. However, all this is in the world "out there." Perhaps there is little that you can do to change the condition or even to remove yourself from the influence of the outside world—yet, you do have a choice!

Life is consciousness. You live in a world of mind. Things may happen around you, in your home, your neighborhood, your city, or in the world. There are times when things may be "laid on you" by chance or by malicious intent, but the only things that count are the things that happen *in* you. Your world, as far as you are concerned, is very definitely formed and shaped by the patterns of your attitudes and feelings. Hard as it is to accept, the truth is: *You make the difference!*

Ella Wheeler Wilcox once sat meditating by the East River in New York Harbor. She was reflecting on the fact that people coming from the same environment turn out so differently. Her attention was turned to watching the great sailing vessels that were pulling up the river to their docks. The poetic flow she recorded in the poem "The Set of the Soul" has much relevancy in our time:

> One ship goes East another West,
> By the self-same winds that blow;
> 'Tis the set of the sail and not the gale
> Which determines the way they go.

Out of the Orient comes this helpful adage: "You can't keep the birds from flying over your head, but you can keep them from building nests in your hair." So, if people get in your hair, or under your skin, you have them there because you chose not to keep them from being there. You may not be able to keep someone from doing or saying certain things. But you certainly do not have to permit him or her to decide for you how you are going to think or feel or act as a result. It is a final choice that is always yours.

A man had been crippled from birth. Early in life his family had done everything to make a basket case out of him. But he would have none of it. He developed a tremendous drive to achieve. He always insisted that there was nothing crippled about his mind, and with this as his resource he worked his way through college. In his career, despite the fact that he has had to hobble painfully about, he has put many people to shame with his accomplishments, and with an unshakable spirit of joy and optimism. He was once asked in an interview, "Hasn't your physical handicap colored your thinking about life and yourself?" And he replied, "Of course it has ... but you see, I always choose the colors!"

So as you face the exigencies of life, you have a choice—you can choose the colors! Things may happen around you, and things may happen to you, but the only things that count are the things that happen *in* you. And here in the realm of your mind, you reign supreme. You can choose to think the way you want. You can turn on the lights, and you can choose the colors. You always have a choice! *You make the difference!*

I. The Importance of You

1. The Need to Be Yourself

Two words of advice we hear often are "Be yourself!" Actually, this is a rather difficult thing to do in view of the pressure that civilization puts on you to conform. But it is equally difficult not to be yourself without paying a terrific price. We haven't always known it but we know it now: the price is paid in terms of unhappiness, restlessness, sickness, sleeplessness, bad dreams, failure, and actual mental illness.

Obviously, certain inhibitions are essential to our happiness and success as members of an increasingly complex society. But somehow in the process of learning to think of other people and their rights, we must discover how to be our unique, true, individual selves instead of just rubber stamps of our parents, teachers, bosses, and friends.

Did you know that no one just like you was ever born before or ever will be again? The geneticist will verify this as true. Thus the question is, "What are you doing about it?" Are you living up to the miracle that is you and you alone? Are you really trying to know yourself, and to release your very own potentialities? Are you making your own unique creative contribution to life or are you just repeating the pattern that has been stamped upon you by others? Are you self-fulfilled?—or self-inhibited? Your health, happiness, and success in life depend to a large extent on your answers to these questions.

Sometimes it is good to check up on yourself with some probing questions: Are you a Republican because your father always voted the straight ticket or because you honestly believe in the present party policies and platform? Are you a Democrat because everyone else in your neighborhood is and it would be awkward to be different? Would you have the courage to change your political affiliation, to change parties, if you honestly felt the other platform to be more realistic and effective?

Did you inherit your religion like the color of your eyes, or does it really express your deepest moral and spiritual convictions? Within your religion are you seeking to find fulfillment and salvation through self-expression and personal development, or is it all a matter of inhibition and self-restraint in conformity with fixed concepts? Would you be willing to change religions if you truly felt that yours no longer met your needs?

And what about your work in life? Are you a minister or actor or doctor or lawyer because your parents wanted you to be, or because your father or mother was one before you, or because you honestly couldn't be happy being anything else? In other words, how much of you is *you* — that wonderful, unique, inimitable you, whose talents, aptitudes, and possibilities are different from any other person alive today?

You have enough personal pride not to neglect taking your bath, combing your hair, and keeping your shoes shined. That same integrity should extend to insisting on your peculiar rights and needs as a person. Don't do and be what others expect you to do and be, no matter how dearly you love them. Be yourself. Unless you live up to the miracle that is *you*, you can never realize your best potentialities.

2. The Great Frontier

Today we know a lot about the world around us, and our knowledge is increasing by leaps and bounds with every passing year. But we know practically nothing about the world within us. The time is coming, and now is, when we will realize once and for all that the great frontier of our day is the quest into inner space.

The Greek philosophers gave a challenge for all ages when they said, "Know thyself." Our most prevalent concept today is that we are innately weak and sinful, bundles of repressions and complexes. It is obvious that this concept comes from viewing people in a static sense. "What I have always done I will always do," and "what has been impossible in the past will always be impossible." But if this were really true we would still be living in caves.

We are told that the genes of the ant provide it at birth with all its tiny faculties fully usable and developed. There is no further growth of power. Unlike the ant, we are born helpless, but with the potential to extend our faculties steadily and augment our grasp and reach. We have the built-in quality of growth and development. And the great lives of history would tend to reveal that there is no limit to what an individual can do or be except the self-imposed limits.

Charles Fillmore, one of the great thinkers of the past century, said in his *Keep a True Lent*, "Man can never discern more than a segment of the circle in which he moves, although his powers and capacities are susceptible of infinite expansion.... The farther he goes into mind, the wider its horizon, until he is forced to acknowledge that he is not the personal, limited thing he appears, but the focus of an infinite idea."

One of the great discoveries of this age is the truth of our infinite potential, and that the purpose of life, as English poet Robert Browning expressed it, is to "open out a way whence the imprisoned splendor may escape." This amazing discovery will eventually have a profound influence in such fields as education, criminology, and psychotherapy.

In an article on "The Psychology of Personal Growth" in *The Atlantic,* Ira Progoff said: "The experiences of Adler, Jung, Rank, and others indicate that neurosis occurs in the modern world not because of repressed fears but because something creative and meaningful is seeking unsuccessfully to express itself in the life of the individual. The frustration of potentiality is the root of neurosis. The implications of this view are large. Man is not a bundle of repressions, but a bundle of possibilities, and the key to therapy lies in reactivating the process of growth."

What does all this mean to you? It means that the great frontier for you today is the world within you. Press forward in your quest! You may well find that deep down within you, far deeper than the so-called complexes of fear and inferiority, is a confident, capable, creative person, the kind of person you want to be, because your very desire is a subconscious perception of your larger potential.

It seems to me that this gives a new implication to the majestic words of Psalm 8:

When I consider thy heavens, the work of
thy fingers, the moon and the stars, which
thou hast ordained; what is man that thou art
mindful of him; and the son of man, that thou
visitest him? For thou hast made him but
little lower than God, and crownest him with
glory and honor. Thou madest him to have
dominion over the works of thy hands;
thou hast put all things under his feet. (vv. 3–6, KJV)

3. Playing the Role

"All the world's a stage, and all the men and women merely
players. They have their exits and their entrances; And one
man in his time plays many parts. . . ." These are the words of
Shakespeare in *As You Like It* — and how true they are! I, for
instance, am a husband, a father, a brother, a neighbor, a writer,
a teacher, an amateur golfer—and I could go on. You, too, are
playing roles all the time, and in every case playing the role well
depends upon a strong self-image, and upon the imagination
to act as if you are what you desire to be.

Remember how easily we pretended to be anything we liked
when we were children? We could be princesses or circus riders,
potentates or beggars, fire-belching dragons or gossamer-winged
fairies. We announced at the beginning of the game just what
we were, and anyone who wanted to play had to accept us in
our chosen role. Of course, we had to act our part up to the
hilt if we hoped to be taken seriously!

It is no different in adult life. The world takes us almost
wholly at our own valuation, accepts us in the role we are
playing to the degree that we play it well. For instance, the
person we think of as successful has, consciously or unconsciously, learned to act the part of a successful individual. And
if we want to be a success we must do the same. How does that
help to make our dream a reality? Frankly, I don't know. (Nor
do I know how or why electricity works.) I only know that it

does work. It has worked for me, and I have seen evidence of it in the lives of thousands of the world's most successful people.

I know a young woman who is considered by everyone to be an exceptionally charming person. She isn't pretty or witty or talented. Yet she has an indefinable charm that makes everyone look twice and long remember. When asked her secret she said:

"Ever since I was a little girl I wanted people to like me. I wanted to be popular, but I had so many handicaps! I wasn't pretty or clever or anything distinctive, so I realized that I must develop something that would make up for what I lacked. As I looked around I realized that the girls who were most popular were not always those who were cleverer, the prettiest, or the best dressed. I studied the problem carefully and I came to the conclusion that it was more important to be considerate than any other thing. The world is so full of selfish, careless, unthinking people, that anyone who tries to be just the opposite—kind, considerate, and gentle—should be a tremendous success.

"I studied the people whom I thought charming. I found that invariably they were persons who said the kindliest things in the kindest way. They were persons who made tact and consideration for the feeling of others the mainspring of their conversation and their actions. I tried their method, and with just a little practice I found myself well on the way to popularity."

And then she adds, "With a little thought one can always say a pleasant, encouraging thing. And the world at large is so hungry for pleasant, encouraging words! While I haven't actually changed myself one particle, I have, by exercising tact and kindness, played a new role, and people have come to accept me as the charming person I wanted to be. I am the same girl, but I pretended to be what I most wanted to be and that is all there is to it!"

If you want the world to accept you in a certain way, carefully create a role and play it to the hilt. In time it will not be sham but real life, and thus you can be what you want to be.

4. You Are Important!

Alfred Adler, one of the fathers of modern psychiatry, said that the desire for recognition, the wish to be significant, is the dominant impulse in human nature.

This is why children are always trying to get attention, to be first. And why, if they can't find prestige and recognition in the harsh world of reality, they seek it in the fairyland of fantasy. And why, in all their dreams, they are somebody important: the knight, the princess, the general, the lady fair.

This desire for recognition explains why we adults are so often taken in by Madison Avenue promotions. "The man of distinction" tells us about the liquor we should drink to get that way. A particular automobile will most certainly make us the envy of all our neighbors. I had a letter the other day from the subscription manager of a newly launched magazine. "As you undoubtedly know," he said, "your name is on several mailing lists in which you are classified as 'highly literate, progressive, interested in world affairs, good literature, and science.' Therefore I know you will be interested in what I have to say." Of course I was interested, since he described me so accurately!

This same urge explains why so many of us are joiners. If we feel unimportant we join lodges or clubs that are. We don uniforms, wear a gaudy button, perhaps become the thirteenth Grand Noble of the Invincible Order of the Mystic Dragon Slayers of the Sea, and so find the thrill of significance. Writer Herbert Doran tells of a man he saw two years after the World's Fair in Chicago had closed still wearing in his lapel a giant-sized button that said, "I attended the Century of Progress." The Fair had taken out of him the humdrum monotony of life as a hired man on the farm, and with a simple token of attendance, for a while at least, he was somebody.

What a monstrous tyrant it can be—this ego that wants to lead the parade. Timid people often become oppressively aggressive. Some fight for a place in the sun by way of envious gossip or malicious criticism; trying to push themselves ahead by pulling others back. Some even become criminals in order to be noticed—like the child who would rather be spanked than ignored. The ends to which we go to achieve significance, to get ahead of the pack, to feel imporant—are both unbelievable and tragic.

Remember, this is an impulse within every person—within you and me. It is an impulse so strong that it quite often is the true motivation behind even those magnanimous gestures of service. Let's take a good look at this need for importance. All the truly great thinkers of all time have agreed that the answer to this need is to realize that you *are* important. You are an essential part of a universal plan, endowed with certain creative talents that the world needs.

Yes, you *are* important! Important to your Creator, and important to the world in which you live. The Man of Galilee once suggested that we should "let our own light shine"—rather than trying to bask in the reflected light of others. You *are* important, and you can find the only satisfaction one ever finds by seeking to live as bravely and helpfully and grandly as you can—coming to be known not so much for what you have done as for what you *are*.

5. Happiness Is Homemade

It has been said that "happiness is the *summum bonum* of existence." Certainly we all desire happiness. It would seem that joy and laughter are gifts of God, but more than we know they are gifts of parents to their children, since it is parents who supply the atmosphere in which the child develops.

No pessimist was ever born. Nature never thought about or intended to create pessimists—they are as artificial as synthetic rubber. The wide-eyed look of expectancy in one's eyes is practically synonymous with childhood. Life is still a miracle. The anything-can-happen quality permeates every moment of the young child's day, and "anything" usually means something nice.

Somewhere along the road of growing up, a child begins to discover that "anything" can sometimes be something-not-so-nice. Still, on the whole, the expectancy of good continues to outweigh the expectancy of bad. Anything can still happen when the sun rises on a new day. What happens in the interval between late childhood and middle life to turn that bubbling, exuberance into the grim adult attitudes is best expressed in the words of a woman who said, "I never expect anything pleasant to happen to me, so I'm not disappointed." Sad as it is, this is a completely adult outlook. No child ever evolved such an attitude.

A prominent neurologist has said, "Raise your children in a cheerful climate." It is important to their childhood, and more important to their mental health in the years to come. The only way to prevent "gloomy Guses" in adulthood is to preserve the natural and spontaneous cheerfulness of the very young. Get the child in the habit of counting the "plus" things that happen out of the blue, such as father coming home early with chocolate bars in his pocket, or mother baking a batch of delicious cookies.

Psychologists say that the individual whose emotional patterns are rooted and grounded in happy expectancy is less likely to fall prey to a philosophy of defeat and pessimism in later years, regardless of what disappointments are encountered. Even serious illnesses involve less risk to the person who does not add the burden of despair to the physical strain under which the body is laboring.

I remember a saying from my childhood, "Little pitchers have big ears." This means that parents should always remember that children are highly impressionable, that parents should restrain themselves for the sake of the children. Negative attitudes and ways of the elders in a family can sap the joyousness of the young. Father comes home after a disappointing business day and hardly opens his mouth at the dinner table, and if he does it is to snap at mother or to grunt at the questions of the youngsters. Mother frets vocally about the high cost of living and about the inadequate salary father is earning, and she too snaps at the children if they have the temerity to act like children.

Children seem to forget these things quickly in their preoccupation with play, but they seep into their consciousness by a process of osmosis and color their emotional attitudes. Years later the pattern begins to repeat itself, and an identification with the earlier home experiences begins to cause trouble. If we are to raise cheerful, emotionally healthy children who will carry the burdens of the future with fortitude, we must maintain happiness and serenity in the home. No good fairy will give the gift of a merry heart in middle life to your child as a christening present. It is up to you now.

6.   Action an Aid to Feeling

Feeling is generally considered to be beyond the control of the will. We often say, "I feel so depressed," with the same tone we use in saying, "It is raining today." There is nothing we can do about it—or so we think. It is just the way things are. However, for a long time some clear-thinking people have been experimenting with the idea of inducing a feeling by indulging in an appropriate action. Shakespeare obviously had this in mind when he said in *Hamlet*, "Assume a virtue, if you have it not." And modern psychology teaches that if you go through the motions, you will come eventually to assume the corresponding emotion.

There is something you can easily experiment with: Put a scowl on your face, grit your teeth, clench your fists, and blurt out ugly sounds, and you will soon develop the feeling of crossness even though you were not cross when you began. Or, on the other hand, lift up the corners of your mouth so as to smile a little, hum a merry tune, and then say with forcefulness, "I feel wonderful." The amazing thing is, no matter how you may have previously felt, you will find yourself a little happier and a little more lighthearted.

If you want to feel sick, act sick: let your shoulders sag and your feet drag; let the corners of your mouth turn down and your eyelids droop; heave a few long sighs. You will begin to imagine all sorts of ailments and symptoms. Experimentation has proven conclusively that by acting the part you can actually make yourself physically sick. Psychosomaticists tell us that many people subconsciously want to be sick for various psychological reasons and thus they induce sickness by acting the part.

Every coin has two sides, so there are exciting implications involved. It must follow that if you want to feel well, or at any rate to feel better even though you are sick, straighten your shoulders, talk with energy about something interesting, get your mind off sickness and symptoms of sickness and start thinking about health and vital life; bring a smile to your lips and face the world gallantly. This can be an actual therapy. Musical therapy, which is used scientifically in many hospitals and institutions, is based on this basic premise. Auto-suggestion and the use of affirmations for health follow the same idea. Be open-minded and adventuresome. Experiment with this idea. See how the action of your body has its effect upon your mental and emotional life.

We affect ourselves by the way we permit ourselves to act. And we affect those around us. One young girl meets her harassed father at the door in the evening with the cheery greeting, "Smile up your face, Dad." It is a reminder to shed the tensions and burdens of the day as he sheds his business suit. With practice anyone can use this simple technique with marvelous results.

This principle is also one for everyday application. When someone with whom you are dealing has a tantrum and becomes abusive, keep your own voice calm, speak in a low tone, sit or stand with all your muscles relaxed, and you will find that you will remain calm, with your emotions at a low pitch. Look gloomy and you feel gloomy, and you will evoke gloom from others. Look cheerful and it will have an inward effect as well as an outward influence. Act lovingly to those with whom it is hard to get along and your heart will feel warm and your relationship will be much smoother.

You cannot do very much to change the world, but you can act the way you want to be, and the way you want the world to be—and, strange as it may seem, such efforts will bear fruit in your own life and in the world around you.

7. Hidden Treasure

Who of us has not at some time thrilled to the story of "buried treasure"? In my youth Robert Louis Stevenson's excit ing book *Treasure Island* was read by young and old alike. Today television portrayals of the classic are still watched with delight. I suspect that we all harbor a secret feeling that somewhere there is a talisman that can change our lives from poverty into plenty, from mediocrity into success. I am sure that it is this feeling that keeps the torch of hope alive for many who otherwise might seem to have little to look forward to in life.

The interesting thing is that most of the really fabulous treasure of the world is passed over in the furious and impetuous race for the quick return. When the cry of "Gold! Gold!" went up in California in 1848, it echoed across the nation. Thousands of people with gold stars in their eyes rushed across the plains. They suffered unbelievable hardships: the ravages of the winter, the dangers of savage Indians, and the wilting heat of desert sun. It was only a comparative few who arrived to sift out a few dollars worth of gold that an even fewer number of them found. And, in their haste they sped right across the present zinc fields of Missouri, the oil fields of Oklahoma, and the wheat fields of Kansas—to say nothing of the fabulous uranium mines in Utah and Nevada.

The richest treasure of life is usually found in completely unexpected places and at unexpected times. A traveler in South Africa noticed children playing with dirty and rough-shaped stones, rolling them as marbles, and throwing them at birds. On closer examination he found them to be huge diamonds in the rough. And that was the discovery of the fabulous Kimberley Diamond Mines—the richest mines in the world. Now, of course, you may never find diamonds in the rough in your back yard, but there are other values, far richer ones, that lie hidden awaiting your discovery and appreciation. Your life right now contains fabulous hidden treasure. We need the discernment to see it and the wisdom to mine it in usable form.

Many of us have within ourselves powers we have not even suspected, and talents we have not developed. One great area of hidden treasure lies dormant in the person who fails to give his all to the work he is doing. He feels that he is doing all he is paid to do, so he allows his greater potential to rust away through disuse. Another type of treasure is hidden in the person who uses his talents in dishonest efforts. This item appeared in the news some months ago: A man's money vault refused to open. It was held by an intricate lock, and the combination failed to work. A search was made for a master locksmith whose sense of touch was so delicate that he could open the vault. A man was found, admittedly one of the most expert. He was found in the state penitentiary, where he was imprisoned for opening doors of others' vaults. Permission was granted to him to exercise his skill on this difficult lock, under guard. He soon mastered it and was then returned to prison. The subtle and delicate skill that might have made him great as a surgeon, musician, or artist, or enabled him in some other capacity to bless the world, had been buried in the moldy yard of thievery.

When we do less than our best, or use our best for less than the best purposes, we cheat ourselves. We need to consider seriously whether we are spending our lives or investing them; whether we are wasting our energies or utilizing them; whether we are burying the treasures of our divinely bestowed talents or circulating them to the betterment of mankind. Take a good look at yourself—you may well be passing over some hidden treasures right now.

8.   What Are You Saying to Yourself?

When I was a youngster I used to know an old rhyme that went something like this: "As I walked by myself I talked to myself, and myself replied to me...." I can only recall those first lines, but I am sure that they have had a lasting influence on my life, because they gave me a clear idea of the self as a definite entity to reckon with.

What we say to ourselves is really tremendously important, for the self is the most suggestible creature in the world. When you make a mistake in your work, do you ever say to yourself, "What a crazy, stupid dunce I am!" Actually it is probably true that your self-suggestion will have a far more harmful effect upon you than anything you did or failed to do.

A little girl who had fallen and hurt her knee and yet was bravely enduring the pain without a whimper, was asked, "How do you keep from crying?" She replied, "Oh, I just say to myself, 'Stop that!' and make myself mind me!" The trouble with most of us is that we are not strict enough with ourselves, not exacting enough. We perform most of the time as if all our responses to life were brought about by a sort of negative reflex action. We become unthinking *re*actors to life, rather than actors. We weakly follow the theme that life seems to set for us, rather than singing our own theme, letting our own light shine.

Perhaps you have been handicapped through your life by timidity or shyness or a sense of inferiority. All right, stop rationalizing your problem by telling yourself that you can't help it, that you have always been that kind of a person. Start saying to yourself: "Other people are too busy to bother about me or to spend their time looking at me; and even if they do, it makes no difference to me, I am going to live in my own way. I am made to do things and I am going to do them." You are no longer a child, so put away those childish thoughts of timidity. Say to yourself, "I am strong and confident. I know what to do and I do it."

The next time you find yourself in a discordant mood, when you feel cross and out of sorts with everybody, when things are rubbing you the wrong way and you aren't getting along with your co-workers or your family, try this little experiment: Stop what you are doing for a few moments and go out of the room, or out of doors if possible. Get out of the atmosphere of the heated situation—and have a "person-to-person" talk with yourself. Like the little girl, say to yourself, "Stop that! What a ridiculous thing for a great, strong person, made to dominate the forces of the universe, to be completely upset, thrown off base by trivial, foolish, insignificant things!" Say to yourself that you are poised and calm, self-possessed and self-respecting. Then go back to your work a new person.

I know a delightful woman who, before she leaves her room in the morning, always looks at herself in the mirror and says, "There is a day of fine opportunities and service ahead of you. And you are going to meet it worthily. I *know* you will, my dear!" I especially like that "I know you will, my dear!" You can almost hear that delightful self of hers responding, "Yes, I'm sure I shall! Anyway, I am going to do my best."

What we say to ourselves is vitally important. It is a good thing to say worthwhile things to yourself and to say them often.

9. What Are You Seeing?

Some years ago I was privileged to see the Passion Play in Oberammergau. It was a never-to-be forgotten experience. Oh, I read the review in *Time* magazine that said the production was inferior, and I heard talk about the commercialism of the little town. But to me the story of the play's origin, the dedication of the people to an ideal through generations, and the beauty of the setting were a great inspiration.

Some time later I was talking with a woman about the play. She remarked that she didn't like it at all. Curious, I asked, "What was it that you didn't like?" She said, "The food was so bad." I recall making some ungracious remark such as, "I didn't go to Oberammergau just to eat." However, this is an interesting insight into human nature.

Often we stand before a splendid sunset, the prismatic brilliance of the cosmic Master's palette flashing in the western sky, and we fret because the wind is disarranging our hair. Or we stand before a great man, who is in himself a victory over environment and circumstances, and mumble about his crude ways and shabby clothes.

I wonder if this tendency to fix our gaze on the superficial and thus to fail to realize life's full potential may be at the root of some of life's greatest frustrations? I wonder too whether, when we come to the "end of our rope," we may be frantically struggling at the end of a thread, unaware that we are securely supported by a cable.

I have a friend who had the jolt of being told unexpectedly that he was to be retired. His department was being eliminated, and his job along with it. As he sat at his desk on his last night at the office with the cold sweat of fear creeping over him, he noted a spider on the desk and unconsciously brushed it off. Suddenly he was watching in amazement as the tiny spider automatically spun a strand to bear its weight, and swung gracefully to the floor. He began to wonder: "Why, if this tiny creature can draw forth from within itself a reserve of substance to meet his emergency, why can I not do as much?"

Suddenly, almost in a flash, he began to see the sunset rather than the wind. Suddenly he knew that the real key to his security was not in his job, but in the source of ideas within him. It was such a transforming realization that he walked out of his office with joy and expectation.

Being forced to do office work had always irked him. He had always secretly longed for the opportunity to do creative writing for a living. Looking at the change from a new viewpoint he could see that *he now had the opportunity.*

So with enthusiasm he plunged into writing. He wrote short stories, essays, and poems. And though he did not attain fame or wealth, he acquired something of much greater value, satisfaction and happiness, and, incidentally, a few checks each month, enough to more than double his half-pay retirement income.

In the challenging changes of your life, what are you seeing? It could well be that you are misreading the lines and failing to see the potential within you and within the experience before you.

A medieval poet once wrote: "That thou seest, man, become too thou must: God, if thou seest God; dust, if thou seest dust."

10. This One Thing I Do

Mark Twain once said, "When I was fourteen years old, my father was so ignorant I hated to have the old man around. But when I was twenty-one, I was surprised to see how much he had learned in only seven years!" It is true that the passing years bring wisdom—and humility. They may bring a decrease in self-assurance, but they bring a larger sense of the abiding values of life.

One of the most important fruits of maturity is the realization of and coming to terms with, "this one thing I do." "This one thing I do"—it spells singleness of purpose, determination, and perseverance. Wrapped up in these five words are some thoughts that may determine in large part whether life is to be a futile, blind experience or a great challenge.

In the first place, when a person says, "This one thing I do," it means that person has made an important decision, has identified life goals, and knows the directions life must take. It also means that individual has found the courage to make a choice even if it means self-sacrifice, or unpopularity in the sight of others.

Many times such decisions are not easy. Albert Schweitzer lived in a hut in the steaming jungles of Africa for fifty years because of a decision; Mark Twain, at sixty years of age and bankrupt, embarked on a lecture tour to earn money to pay his debts because of a decision; Abraham Lincoln carried the terrible burden of a nation engaged in civil war—because he made a decision.

In the second place, when a person says, "This one thing I do," it is a commitment in unmistakable terms to a life with singleness of purpose. Many of us would like to be great in some field, to be recognized and appreciated. But are we really willing to achieve that goal by the hardest work, the longest hours, and the greatest sacrifice? Voltaire once said of a man that he was like an old-fashioned oven: always heating but never cooking anything. Too many lives are like that.

Many of us almost reach the boiling point—almost but not quite. It may well be that the element needed to bring us to a boil is the determination not only to be successful but to live a noble life, to live for ideals and objectives that will outlast our own life.

In Marc Connelly's play *Green Pastures*, Noah says to the Lord, "I ain't very much, but I'm all I got." Well, you're all you've got. The question is "What are *you* going to do with what you've got?" Will you use yourself to make life richer, better, nobler? Certainly you will not, unless you make a decision to do so, and unless beyond that decision you set your sights on "this one thing I do."

This, then, is the decision and the one single and great objective in life: to take whatever occupation or profession you may be in—doctor, businessman, farmer, dentist, banker, attorney, schoolteacher, housewife—and to live life greatly, nobly; to live for those ideals that will outlast your own life. The person who so lives will be able to say, "I have fought a good fight, I have finished my course, I have kept the faith." And more than this, that person will be happy and fulfilled, at peace within and with the world.

11.   The Woodcarver and the Bear

The story is told that a woodcarver was finishing up a very lifelike figure of a bear that he had carved out of a block of wood when his young son asked if he might have a block of wood to carve out a bear. The father gave him the wood and told him to go ahead. Some time later, when the child had gotten the block down to a last thin sliver, he looked up and said, "Father, I couldn't find any bear in my block of wood."

The only bear that anyone will ever find in any block of wood is the one that has been first created in the mind's eye. Our lives are the direct result of the mental image we habitually hold. We cannot be more or less than we see ourselves as being. And, strangely enough, what we see in others, by and large, is a reflection of the bear in our own mind.

Some time ago a story on television depicted a man who hated people; a man who, as he rode the bus to work in the morning, saw only an ugly, snarling, pushing mass of humanity. When he entered the large office building where he worked, everyone, from the man behind the newsstand to the elevator operator, was frowning and gruff. Even the good-natured office boy managed to spill coffee on him every morning. All the man could think of was how much he hated the human race.

Then the man read a book about the power of concentration. He found that by concentrating he could make all the people in his world disappear. He rode to work on an empty bus; he entered a silent and empty office building; he rode an empty elevator; he entered an office with empty desks. There were no people anywhere, no one but himself.

At first he relished the fact that he was the only person in his world; but as the day wore on, he had to admit that the experience was not as pleasant as he thought it would be. Then an idea struck him! He would bring the people back; but they would be people just like himself, as he was the only person he could stand. So the next morning he entered a bus full of people, all looking like him and frowning. In his office he was surrounded by people who looked like him and who looked as if they couldn't stand the sight of him. Of course, he did not like this state of affairs, and he finally decided that people, just people as they are, made up a better world than any he could create.

The story is a fantasy, of course, but the important point it makes is that we project our bad feelings to others and see them as disgruntled or unhappy, without realizing that it is we ourselves with whom we are dissatisfied. If we don't like people, if we think that people don't like us, the reason is that we don't like ourselves. We might change everyone else, but we would still have to live with ourselves, and until we change ourselves, we cannot be happy or at peace.

You can carve a bear out of a block of wood, but first you must get the picture of it in your own mind. You may be amazed at how your life will change, how your relationships will improve, how people will actually appear different, when you begin to look for the good in yourself and in others. And even as the child might some day become a skilled woodcarver like his father if he follows his example and keeps trying, so you can become an artist in the fine art of drawing the very best out of everyone with whom you associate.

II. Thinking Makes It So

12. Thinking About Thinking

Someone has said, "What is life but what a person is thinking of all day?" What do you think of all day long? Are your thought images merely impressions thrust upon you from the outside world? What is your first waking thought? Perhaps a reluctant admission that you have to get up. Why this reluctance? Is it that the business of life—going to work, satisfying your boss, earning money for bills, eating, dressing, pleasing people, accepting responsibilities—has become a burden to be met only with dread? It may depend on how you meet it, upon your attitude.

Where do we get our thoughts? Certainly this depends upon us. It is possible to be an original thinker, to think only what we want to think. But most of us most of the time are second-hand thinkers. We pick up thoughts in the papers, where, for instance, the National Safety Council announces that so many hundred people will die on the highways over a given weekend. We absorb thoughts from people around us, like the man in the bus who loudly announces, "If the financial picture continues to look bad, some of us will soon be facing layoffs from work. There are some bleak days ahead."

Negative suggestions from the world around us! It is up to us to accept them or let them slide harmlessly over our heads. Why do we accept them? Because we are filled with fear—the fear of the world is upon us. The world that has gone through so much travail and pain in its myriad misconceptions.

In the past thousands of years there have been famines, pestilences, and wars, yet every day of every year the sun has shone, the rain has refreshed the earth, or the snow has enwrapped the sleeping buds of the following spring. We do not remember these things because they are our heritage. We take them for granted.

For twenty years a certain family slept securely in their beds every night. And then a burglar entered and robbed them.

After that they were terribly afraid every night. They forgot the twenty years of security because of only one night of insecurity.

We take up the morning paper to see what the news is, and instantly our eyes are glued upon the horrifying description of the latest murder. We read with uneasiness the reports of our changing relations with other nations. The writers who describe these things are experts at picturing gruesome details or in bringing out the most negative aspects. Our thoughts begin to leap. No one is safe anymore! There are no more honest people! Are we going to become involved in another war? A hundred thoughts flit through our minds—and again we are possessed by the demon fear.

If life is what you are thinking about all day, then if you want a harmonious and effective life, you had better see to it that you give your mind the right diet for breakfast, and keep your mind centered on positive things all day long.

A favorite poem of mine says:

> You never can tell what your thoughts will do,
> In bringing you hate and love;
> For thoughts are things, and their airy wings
> Are swifter than carrier doves.
> They follow the law of the universe
> Each thing must create its kind
> And they speed o'er the track to bring you back
> Whatever went out from your mind.
>
> Ella Wheeler Wilcox

13. The World You Live In

What is the world like to you at this moment—your world? Actually, no two of us live in the same world at any time. Your neighbor may be having a headache, so his or her present world is pain-clouded. Your child may be out playing in a world of all laughter and fun. Your business associate may be poring over charts and statistics, planning a new campaign—a world both thoughtful and serious.

And you—what of you? Is your world happy, harmonious, healthy? One thing is sure. If anything is making you less than happy right now, it is not likely to be doing so a week, a month, or a year from now. Can you remember what was bothering you a year ago today? Of course not. Your world is constantly changing, and thus a tremendous technique that can give you mastery over life's ups and downs is this: in the face of whatever seems to be irritating or worrisome, say emphatically, "This too shall pass."

You see, your world is made in the image and likeness of whatever you most consistently believe in or give your attention to. It follows then that you cannot think one thing and get another. If you are thinking trouble, you will get trouble. Fortunately, the reverse is also true by reason of the same law. If you think health, joy, peace, plenty, and love, you will get more of them.

History and the experiences of everyday life bear this out. The man who built the Bastille was later imprisoned in it. The carpenter who built Boston's first set of stocks was accused of overcharging for the job and became its first prisoner. A rigid ecclesiastic invented the Iron Cage, a torture chamber so constructed that the victim could neither stand upright nor lie down in it. He later spent eleven years in his own invention.

This is true in your life and mine. We are confined in prisons of our own making, caught in traps we ourselves have laid. Fortunately there is a happy side to the matter. Change your thinking and you change events. What are you thinking about: sickness or health? animosities or friendships? recession or prosperity? Your answer determines the state of your world.

Modern medical scientists are now very sure that most of our health ills are individually chosen in accordance with the exact pattern of our dominant thoughts and emotions. Experienced doctors can even look at the kind of person you are and predict what ailments you are likely to be subject to! Arthritics, medical experts say, are usually harboring self-pity and resentment, and this causes the joints to stiffen into rigidity. Stomach ulcers, some doctors say, come from excessive dependency, which the victim attempts to cover up in favor of appearing more independent than is really the case. This is what the doctors call "organ language." In short, the organs of the body try to tell us that something is wrong with our thinking and our feelings. Our ills then, to modify the words from the Book of Common Prayer, are "outward and visible signs of an inward and spiritual distress."

Take time to study yourself and your own personal world. If you are not satisfied with what you see, set about to make some changes. Change your dominant thoughts, your outlook, your viewpoint. Change what you believe in and give your attention to. As author and publisher Elbert Hubbard put it, "Man's not what he thinks he is, but what he thinks, he is."

14. It's What's Inside That Counts

There have been times in the lives of all of us when some challenging change or misfortune has deprived us of something that seemed all but irreplaceable. This is a most severe test of one's inner stability. Many individuals have been helped in such crises by the simple philosophy of American poet Emily Dickinson, who wrote, "Things may happen around you, and things may happen to you, but the only things that really count are the things that happen in you." You can't change what has happened, but you can change your thoughts about it, and it is right here where you have mastery over your life.

When an exploding bomb blew off the hands of paratrooper Harold Russell, he felt that his life was over. He had been looking forward to returning to his old job as apprentice to a butcher, thinking that with luck he might someday become manager of a butcher shop. Suddenly—no hands, no apprenticeship, no managership. No future. No hope. He was licked.

It was not that the accident made him helpless. Army doctors had fitted him with ingenious prosthetic appliances, metal fingers that were so artfully contrived that he could delicately manipulate even the smallest articles with the instrument dexterity of a skillful surgeon. With his artificial fingers he could operate a typewriter, shoot a target rifle, light a cigarette, and even thread a needle. He was far from being helpless, but he was hopeless, which was worse. And why? Not because of what had happened *to* him, but what had happened *in* him. He thought that he had become a freak.

He felt that strangers would regard him—a man without real hands—as a pitiful or unpleasant curiosity. He was confident of his ability to use a knife and fork, but he was ashamed to do it publicly. What would other diners think of him? What would the waitress think? The man who had not feared to jump from a speeding airplane was now afraid to walk into a restaurant.

When he was at lowest ebb, psychologically, he was invited to make a training film to help other amputees. He was given the opportunity to use his misfortune to help others similarly deprived. He buried his pride, his vanity, his concern about what other people might think of him. The rest is history. He signed a contract to perform in the motion picture *The Best Years of Our Lives* and became the only actor ever to receive two Motion Picture Academy Awards for an outstanding performance in a single film. And out of this new experience evolved a life rich in social contacts with all manner of people who are trying to make this a better world in which to live.

Asked whether he held any regrets about his condition, Harold Russell said, "No. My deprivation has been my greatest blessing." And he added, "What counts is not what you have lost but how you use what you have left." In other words, it is not what happens *to* you, but what happens *in* you that determines the effect that life's experiences will have upon you. Everyone has within the stature to stand tall in the face of any experience if he or she will only decide to do so. Obviously each individual must win many inner battles and ignore the temptation to give in to self-pity and to wallow in the sympathy of others.

To experience loss is human, and certainly life is change, which inevitably means loss and separation and occasionally deprivation. But to transmute such experiences into an artistic, educational, and spiritual opportunity is the highest use of one's divine capabilities. Yes, it's what's inside that counts.

15. How to Reverse Adversity

I think I can safely say that no one is entirely free from trouble of some kind, because life is change, and whenever there is change there is the tendency to resist. And it is the resistance to change that becomes the problem—the adverse reactions to changing circumstances. It is important, first of all, to remember that a problem may exist, but it is not permanent; something *can* be done about it.

You have limitless potentialities within you to be discovered. The challenges of life are often the best avenue to discovery. The tragedy may become a blessing, and the disadvantage may become an advantage. What is life all about anyway, except the opportunity for growth and development as a person? There is no better place or circumstance in which to do the growing you need than right in the face of the thing that you may have been calling a handicap or obstacle.

Develop the art of looking for the advantage in disadvantage, for the good in all changing experiences. Take a sheet of paper and list all the advantages you can find in the particular challenge that disturbs you. Keep trying. You will find them. This will direct your thought toward nonresistance and faith.

The real adversity is the adverse reaction to the experience—not the experience itself. Thus the real problem is in your mind, in your attitudes. Work with this thought, for if the problem is in your mind, it is right where you *can* deal with it. In physics there is a law of reversibility that states that the expression of force is reversible—for instance, magnetism engenders electricity, but also, electricity engenders magnetism. Whatever experience we face evokes a certain feeling, and if that feeling can be reproduced in the absence of the experience it will tend to bring the experience back again in fact and expression.

For example, if you are unemployed, reverse the adverse thoughts. You may have been dwelling on the belief that you are "destitute," "down and out," "a failure." Change this to the idea that you are ready for work, your pocketbook is ready to be filled. Think activity, movement; envision work and service. Get the *feel* of work, of success—and you will see it come to pass. Reverse your adversity by changing your adverse thoughts and feelings about the experience. When you feel down and out, limited, or depressed, you can reverse the whole process by doing the things that will make you feel happy and successful. Put on your best clothes, set your table with your best china, linen, and silver—things you have saved for a special occasion— "this is it!" You will soon get the feeling of success, which will trigger a very definite force toward that end.

Often the need is to get some altitude in your thinking. Here is an interesting and helpful technique: Take a note pad and draw a horizontal black line through the center of each page, with a small plus sign at the left above the line and a small minus sign just below. Put this pad on your desk or by the phone—wherever you may be apt to make notes about things that have happened or of things to be done. Challenge yourself to decide honestly, before putting each note on paper, if your thought about it is positive or negative. For instance, you have an appointment to meet a client, and you are seriously apprehensive about the results. Put the note below the line on the pad. If you are looking forward to the interview, put it above the line. At the close of the day, go through the notes and transpose all minuses into pluses by reversing the adverse thoughts, thinking of some positive attitude to hold about the situation. The cosmic law is that if the thought is positive, something good will come. No matter what has happened or is yet to come, you can never afford to let your adverse thoughts stand—reverse the adversity by changing the thought. Try this technique and it will work wonders for you.

16. The Right Angle

A photographer of great skill, whose pictures command a good price in the magazine market, was trying to get a dramatic picture of a lovely old church. He had walked about the building two or three times, surveying it from every angle. An amateur photographer commented on his great care, and the artist said,

"In every situation there is one right angle from which to shoot—one spot on which to fix your camera lens if it is to get the best picture. Almost any building, person, or scene can be made into a beautiful picture if you get a shot from the right angle."

This right angle is often thought of as the lucky angle. We all know people who seem to enjoy good fortune in all situations. When they start an enterprise it succeeds; when they travel they meet interesting people and have a wonderful time. The Egyptians have a saying: "He falls in the river and comes up with a fish in his mouth." To the person who is good-luck prone, every problem seems to be the springboard to something good, every disappointment leads to what Horace Walpole refers to as "serendipity." That's a ten-dollar word that means the gift of making lucky or unexpected "finds" by accident.

Pitirim Sorokin, former Chairman of Harvard University's Sociology Department, said in his book *Man and Society in Calamity*, after surveying the history of humanity's encounters with trouble and disaster, that some persons meet tragedy and suffer the "disintegration of personality," or as we would say it, "they fall apart at the seams." On the other hand, says Sorokin, there are other men and women who, pushed against the wall, see their troubles as a challenge to their faith and courage. They make their troubles work for them and the harder they fall, the higher they bounce.

It all seems to depend upon finding the right angle. If we find the right angle any trouble can stab us awake and lead us to personal serendipity in the discovery of undreamed of possibilities in ourselves. But what is the right angle? Redundant as it sounds, the right angle is the conviction born of faith that there *is* a right angle. It is the attitude similar to that of the photographer who knew there was one right angle and who kept looking until he found it. The right angle from which to view life and all of its challenging changes is the conviction that "all things work together for good"; the faith that somewhere in the problem is the means of becoming a bigger, better person.

Now of course tragedy, handicap, and misfortune do not spontaneously reveal the right angle. But anyone who insists upon finding that angle, that inherent good, will surely find it.

Gene Neely was living aimlessly until a shotgun deprived him of one arm. Somehow this crippling accident seemed to charge this young fellow with a burning mission to prove that a man with one arm can do anything that a man with two arms can do. Unbelievably, under the stress of his challenge, he became an All-American football player at Dartmouth College. Somehow he found the right angle.

It is a good thing to remind yourself constantly that no matter what you see, you see good in embryonic form. Someone will find the right angle and turn it to some good. Why not you? Form the habit of looking for the right angle in every experience, and in time everyone will refer to you as that lucky-so-and-so. Only you will know it is not luck—but the right angle, the realization born of faith that "all things work together for good."

17. The Power of Suggestion

"Every day, in every way, I'm getting better and better." These are the words made famous over fifty years ago by a French psychotherapist, Emilé Coué. They have been ridiculed and joked about, but the startling thing is that as the years have passed, more and more practitioners in the fields of medicine, psychology, and religion are coming to accept some of Dr. Coué's findings.

Emilé Coué frankly admitted that he possessed no healing powers, but that each person who came to him had within all the remedies necessary for well-being. He pointed out that most of us carry in our minds innumerable frightening images that have been accumulating since childhood. Our powers have been dammed up by the suggestions of others, by what we have read, and by various experiences. He said that we have become hypnotized into a state of helplessness, so he taught the practice of affirming to oneself a belief in one's inner strength, harmony, and well-being. He believed that it was possible for anyone to wake up the giant within by the daily practice of repeating some dynamic, stimulating statement.

Today, more and more people are realizing the importance of positive mental attitudes. The popularity of books on "positive thinking" is evidence of widespread interest on a national scale. Today there are whole organizations devoted to helping people to change their patterns of thought from negative to positive.

The power of suggestion is a deep and complicated area of research. It is a subject that cannot and should not be generalized about. The power of suggestion can be used destructively as well as constructively. It is used in advertising and it is used in political propaganda. However dangerous it may be in some cases, we cannot, or at least should not, discount its importance in impressing things on our subconscious mind that can help us to be happier, healthier, and more confident and successful. Of course to affirm a thing does not make it true, but affirmation can direct our minds and our thoughts toward that which is true, and can develop our own faith in the truth of that which is true.

I believe strongly that each one of us is and should be the engineer of his or her own life. What we allow our minds to dwell upon determines most of the things that happen to us. And if this is true, then the concepts of Emilé Coué may not be as far out as they have seemed. It certainly would not hurt any of us to do a little experimenting with affirmation and mental suggestion.

What is it that you want to do or be? Affirm that you can have or become what you want. Get it strongly in your mind as a possibility. Think about all of its aspects. See yourself receiving it, using it, and make it as real as you can in your imagination. Then keep on affirming it until it becomes a reality.

Call this mental suggestion, call it Couéism, call it practical religion, or metaphysics, or just common sense—there is a possibility that you can release some of your new potentialities in this way, and begin to use the powers of your subconscious mind confidently and dynamically. It could be that Emilé Coué and many of the more contemporary advocates of mental suggestion and affirmation have touched upon a vital key to effective living. "Day by day in every way I am getting better and better."

18. The Fine Art of Changing One's Mind

It is a strange thing how we have picked on the idea that a woman is forever changing her mind, and hold it up to ridicule. The truth is that every step of progress in the intellectual world has been gained because people have had the courage to change their minds. The people who have done the really great things throughout history were people who developed to a fine art the faculty of changing their minds gracefully and effectively.

Somehow there seems to be a popular aversion to the very idea of changing one's mind when the larger interests of life are involved. The person who will change clothes as a matter of everyday custom or adjust to changes of weather or social environment seems to think it somehow disgraceful to change political party or religion. Why is this? Why are we so jittery about any change in our fundamental beliefs? I think I can see three possible reasons:

1. We think of our beliefs not as natural functions of our mind, subject like every other natural endowment to readjustment and growth, but rather as inherited standards to which we must conform all our thinking. So instead of looking upon a change of mind as an indication of growth, we are apt to regard it as a mark of uncertainty or failure.

2. Our beliefs tend naturally to group us in certain classes. This is notably true of our moral and religious convictions, and to some extent, of our ethical and esthetic judgments. We have, by reason of our beliefs, identified with a certain group: the club, the church, the political party. The temptation to change our views evokes a feeling of guilt, of being disloyal to the group. The fear of being different, of isolation, of walking alone, prods us into conformity.

3. When we begin to tamper with our beliefs, we find that they are not separate or separable, but are interwoven with other beliefs. You just can't cast aside a belief as you could pull out a loose brick in a wall and put another in its place. We find that we have to deal with life as a whole, and every major conviction throughout life is an intricate part of our whole outlook. Thus often we hold onto a belief because of the fear that it will destroy the whole house. This fear often keeps a person from reading or studying in areas that are considered unorthodox, for there is a danger of contamination, a fear that infection will spread through the whole person.

Yet, isn't it true that the whole process of growing up in life is a simple matter of outgrowing our clothes, our playthings, and our immature concepts? At every step of our onward progress we are bidding good-bye to some cherished belief, or ideal, or prejudice that seemed to be such an important part of our mental outfit.

It seems to me that one is not fully matured and ready to make a contribution to life until the fine art of changing one's mind has been developed. All learning, all science, all religion should be open-ended. We should form the habit of qualifying our convictions with the thought: "This I believe to be true, as far as I can now see." But as we come to the horizon, let us develop the nonresistance to change, and let go of old threadbare concepts in favor of that which is more all-inclusive. Unless we develop this art of changing our minds, we shall decline, as multitudes have done, to the dead level of cynical pessimism.

19. Creative Imagination

One of the sad things about growing up is that we adults too often lose our ability to pretend, to imagine. To the young child imagination is a magic door that leads to thrills, excitement, and happiness. When we deny children the full exercise of their imaginations in our efforts to have them face the facts of life, we may close the magic door for them, perhaps for all time. The imaginative child of early years often becomes the creative genius of later years.

It is the imaginative people who lead the world. Every great work in the world first has its place in the imagination. Shakespeare in *A Midsummer-Night's Dream* describes the creative process that scientists, inventors, poets, musicians, and painters experience:

> And, as imagination bodies forth
> The forms of things unknown, the poet's pen
> Turns them to shapes, and gives to airy nothing
> A local habitation and a name.

It is a fact that imagination takes hold of what seems to be "airy nothing" and makes something permanent out of it. Of course, there is no "airy nothing." There is a universal energy everywhere present that is sensitive to human thoughts. Whether we know it or not we are continually forming and shaping this energy and substance through our thoughts.

If one is about to build a bench, one must first picture in mind the kind of bench it should be. An *engineer* who has a contract to build a bridge must first become what we might call an *imagineer*. The intangible work, building a clear mental picture of the job, must be done before the tangible bridge can be built. The imagination must "body forth" the need for a bridge, and "give to airy nothing" the shape and the name of a bridge.

We often use the expression, "It's just a figment of my imagination." But I wonder what civilization would be like if it were not for the many "figments" that led to all progress and development. Columbus's new world was a "figment." Fulton's steamboat was a "figment." Edison's incandescent lamp was a "figment." It may well be that your life and mine could reach undreamed of heights of accomplishment if we were to cultivate the imagination in a creative and positive sense.

Of course, the imagination does some strange things to us. A group of men, hard-pressed to get hotel reservations and in desperation, accepted a room that had been used for a storage room. There was no way to open the window. In the night, unable to sleep for lack of ventilation, one of the men in anger threw a vase at the window and broke the glass. They then slept peacefully through the night. In the morning, on surveying the damage, they realized that the window was still intact and tightly shut—the vase had broken a mirror on the wall. The fresh air was only a figment of their imagination. But the fact is that they did sleep soundly. This type of "figment" suggests the placebo of the physician, when a sugar-coated *nothing* is given to a patient as an avenue to find peace when there is nothing wrong but "chronic imaginitis."

Looking for a moment at success—everyone wants to be a success. But not very many people believe that they can succeed. Why not create a "figment" of imagination? As Dorothea Brande suggests, "Act as if it were impossible for you to fail." One very successful industrialist says, "It is just as easy to imagine yourself successful as it is to imagine failure, and far more interesting." Creative imagination!

20. Can You Imagine That?

"Can you imagine that?" We have all expressed this thought at one time or another. But I wonder if we have always realized its implications? It is through the right and wise use of creative imagination that man achieves great ends. The great people of history did the creative works they did precisely because they *could* imagine them first in their minds.

We think of Enrico Caruso as the world's greatest tenor. It is hard to imagine him struggling for recognition but at one time he was terribly discouraged. He had been singing for several years in minor opera companies in small towns in Italy. His voice was so limited in range and power that he was given only small roles and not very many of those. He had no money, no influential friends. Students used to laugh at him and call him the tenor with the glass voice because it broke so easily on high notes. His teachers had all told him that he could never hope to amount to anything as a singer.

Finally he decided that when the troupe completed its tour, he would return to Naples and get into some other kind of work. Then a miracle happened. The leading tenor left without notice. They asked Caruso to go on and sing *Rigoletto*. He knew he must do it, because the audience would have to be turned away if he didn't, and the performers would all lose the pay that was coming to them. "Sure, I'll do it, why not?" he said to himself. After all, he had nothing to lose. No matter how badly he failed, it couldn't make any difference now. There is an old Italian saying, "When you've rolled in the gutter, an extra splash or two of mud makes little difference."

So Caruso got into his costume, put on the greasepaint, and began to say to himself, "Enrico, for tonight you must pretend that you are a real artist, a leading tenor." He kept looking at himself in the mirror, saying, "You are an artist. A leading tenor." So engrossed was he in the image of success he was creating that he gave his voice no thought. Ordinarily he went on stage nervous and tense, expecting his voice to break. But not this time. He was actually acting the part of a successful tenor. He went through the opening scenes without a flaw, and after the first aria, he received a tremendous ovation. At the end of the first act, he had three curtain calls. At that moment he became a great artist. He had envisioned himself being a leading tenor—even only for a single role—and his crushed and broken spirit was reborn. It spread its wings and cried for all the world to hear, "You can, you can, you can."

You too can build an image of the person you want to be, the role you want to play, the confidence and creativity you want to express. Look at yourself in the mirror and tell yourself, "You can be the confident and capable person you desire to be. You can." See it as being a very real potential. Believe in your ability to fulfill the image, you will achieve fulfillment. There is a principle involved: Conceive a thing in your mind or imagination, believe in your ability to realize it, and you will achieve it in your experience.

This power of imagination is very real, and very influential. On the other side, it can work against your best interests, and often does just that. Many of the problems in our lives are problems essentially because we see them in that way. Many of the ills to which people seem heir exist only in our imagination. The modern field of psychosomatic medicine deals entirely with illnesses that are emotionally induced. A classic example is the soldier who was "wounded" and brought into a field hospital for an operation. His pulse was low, his heartbeat was feeble, and his entire countenance was steeped with death. The operating surgeon removed his coat and a piece of shrapnel fell to the floor. The soldier saw the shrapnel on the floor and it suddenly dawned on him that what he had thought was a fatal wound was simply the impact of the bullet against his belt buckle. In the stress of fear, he had built up a concept of death and it nearly destroyed him.

The principle is: What you see, you become. If you have a problem with your health or finances or human relations, what resolution would you like to see manifest? "Can you imagine that?" If you can imagine it, actually see it in your mind and then believe in it as a reality, you may be amazed at how quickly it will come to pass.

21. How to Manage Your Emotions

Everyone wants to be happy, and when conditions are not conducive to happiness, we have unhappiness. For instance, it is hard to be happy with a splitting headache. So it is easy to conclude that the illness caused the unhappiness. But you must begin to realize that your emotional states determine the well-being of your body just as surely as they reflect it. In other words, it is completely possible that unhappiness may actually cause illness.

It is not enough to say, "All right, my problem is emotional, but my headaches are just as severe, and my body pains are real." Sure, they are real. But you must begin to realize that emotions can be managed. A little inventory of emotional disturbances will reveal that over a period of twenty-four hours most of the things that upset you were mighty little things: the coffee was cold, the service was slow, the cuff-link rolled under the bed, the bus broke down. Face yourself with the question: "All right, so these things happened! Why should everything always come my way? These things happen in the best-regulated life. Instead of expecting the world to be stable for me, I must determine that I am going to find poise and stability within myself."

At the same time, we mustn't oversimplify the challenges of life—there are many problems to be encountered; many adjustments to be made. Mental health is simply the ability to maintain emotional control in the face of life's stresses. As a matter of fact the basis of mental disease is the loss of such control. Every time you are consumed by resentment, driven by frustration, unnerved by worry or anger, overcome by fear, you are suffering from a kind of mild mental illness, so don't take such things lightly.

What is the best way to control your emotions and thus control your life? First of all: *believe* that you can; believe that you were intended to master and use your emotions and not be mastered by them. Then re-emphasize that *life is lived from within out*—that you can't always change the world around you, but you can and must take control over the world within. Your fears, resentments, angers, and even grief come because you feel that the instability of life around you threatens your very existence. Change that whole picture—alter the self-image from an individual who reacts to every sort of outer stimuli to one whose purpose in life is to release a steady flow of poised energy from the infinite potential within.

Emphasize to yourself that you are not a victim of circumstances at the mercy of anything and everything that happens around or to you. You are an inward-centered person, with the power to master your mind and emotions. In the realm of mind you are king—here you have control—or you should have. The winds will blow, and they may not always blow in the way you want to go. You can't regulate the winds, so there is no use trying, and no use complaining about them. But you can set the sails and tack right into the teeth of the gale—and go on.

This kind of emotional control doesn't come without effort. You will have to work constantly to create and sustain an inward spirit that is inwardly fed and is not dependent on conditions in the world. Samuel Johnson said, "It is worth a thousand pounds to have a bright outlook." Once a young girl became totally blind. She wandered in the depths of depression for quite awhile. Then one day an inspiration came to her: "Think light." She couldn't see light, but she began to "think light." She never recovered the vision of her eyes, but she developed a tremendous mental vision. She found her mind working more clearly than ever before, and she built a new life for herself. Think light. When you think dark, things seem hopeless. When you think light, there is always the possibility for good in every circumstance.

22. Keeping Up with Yesterday

I remember seeing in a museum some years ago a couple of dinosaur eggs. It was quite an attraction, because you couldn't help but think, "Just imagine, the mother laid those eggs millions of years ago, and here they are untouched!"

Actually, for the dinosaur in question, those eggs represent complete failure. After all the trouble of laying them, nothing ever came of them. Thinking of them in this way, we can all find plenty of dinosaur eggs in our lives—desires and ideals that have been postponed and neglected through procrastination.

Procrastination is the art of keeping up with yesterday. It is the unconscious practice of keeping one's desires, ideals, and opportunities as museum pieces, as dinosaur eggs that never hatch out. In a sense it could be said that tomorrow will be the most wonderful day in history, for that is the day when most of us say we are going to begin doing better.

I suspect that there are many dinosaur eggs lying around your home. Someone said, "Give a man a household job and he goes through three phases: contemplating how it will be done, contemplating when it will be done, and contemplating." It is absolutely wonderful, the ingenuity of the human mind in finding reasons for putting off until tomorrow the things that ought to be done today. This is probably one of the most important factors in modern life.

I have a friend in business who has more responsibilities and less care or worry than anyone I have ever known. I asked how he was able to do it. He said it was due to his invariable practice of clearing off his desk by the close of the day in order to begin the following day clear and fresh. A simple enough key! But, you see, one of the great challenges in life is the feeling of being weighed down by all the things we have to do. We allow things to accumulate not only on our desks but in our minds. Because we are worrying about how to get all of them started and completed, we start none and thus nothing is done. We need always to remember that a big job is simply a handful of little jobs, any one of which we could do easily, if we just begin, and do one thing at a time.

To begin is often half the battle. Theodore Roosevelt used to say: "Do what you can with what you have right where you are." How often we say, "Next winter I am going to study French," or "I will look for that job next week." When we say, "I will do it tomorrow," it usually means never! If there is anything we want to do or should do, now is the time to begin.

The philosopher-poet Goethe wrote some lines that you might want to memorize, or at least put on a card on the desk or over the kitchen sink or on the bathroom mirror, where you will continually be reminded of it. It goes like this: "Are you in earnest? Seize this very minute. Whatever you can do, or dream you can, begin it. Boldness has genius, power, and magic in it."

If indolence or the pressure of seemingly overloaded days has developed in you the habit of putting off until tomorrow what should be done today; if, like Scarlett O'Hara of *Gone with the Wind*, you meet the great crises of life with the thought, "I won't think about it now. I'll think about it tomorrow"; if you are postponing the good you desire by thinking, "Someday I will have it" or "someday I will start it"; if you are keeping up with yesterday and nursing stale dinosaur eggs, then make a commitment right now to rid yourself of the habit. Remember, "whatever you can do, or dream you can, begin it. Boldness has genius, power and magic in it."

III. Getting Along with People

23. The One Creative Force

"Some day—perhaps soon—humankind will learn what individuals have always known: that love is the only truly creative force in the world." Those are the words of sociology professor Pitirim Sorokin.

Here is a man who went through two of the harshest periods in history, those immediately before and after the Revolution in Russia—a man who had every reason to hate, but who said, "The thing I remember most about those days was love." He said, "Love acted as an antidote. Its force created little islands of health amid great sickness."

He told of one simple yet amazing experience. He was attending school in a nearby village, walking to school through the snow with his toes showing through the soles in his boots. The teacher was a gaunt young man who had no reason to give special thought to this son of a traveling painter who would disappear one morning as suddenly as he had come. But the teacher looked at the lad's torn shoes and without a word went to the closet and took out his second pair of boots. "But you" Sorokin said, "what will you wear?" "Keep them," the teacher said. "Why should I have two pairs when you have none?"

Sorokin said that it is this incident that gave him hope for the contemporary world. We are living in another era of violence and hate, and yet, because of what he had seen, and because of the love that could always be found coming from people in the midst of their deepest troubles, he had high hopes for the world of today. Surely, it is love that has always brought out the best in people; it is love that has always been the silent and yet dynamic influence in the lives of individuals, and through them upon the world.

More than a quarter century ago a college professor had his sociology class go into the worst slum area in Baltimore and get case histories of two hundred young boys. When the students returned, the professor asked them to write at the bottom of each information sheet their prediction of each boy's future. Without exception, the students wrote words to the effect: "He hasn't got a chance." Twenty-five years later another sociology professor came across the earlier study and decided to follow it up. He told his class about the questionnaire and asked his students to find out what had happened to those boys. The class did so. With the exception of 20 boys who had moved away or died, the students learned that 176 of the remaining 180 had achieved more than ordinary success as lawyers, doctors, businessmen and so on.

The professor was astounded. What had caused this unexpected result? He decided to pursue the subject further. Fortunately, all the men were in Baltimore and he was able to speak to each one. "How do you account for your success?" he asked. Each replied with feeling, "There was a teacher." Finally the University professor decided to pursue the query further. What was the magic formula the teacher had to pull those boys out of the slums into success? Again, fortunately, the teacher was still alive. He went to see her. He asked the elderly but still alert lady her secret, her magic formula. The teacher's eyes sparkled and her lips broke into a gentle smile. "It's very simple," she said, "I loved those boys."

Where there was no chance, love found a way. Perhaps we should take Professor Sorokin's words seriously—"that love is the only truly creative force in the world."

24. How to Get Along with People

If you read the funny papers, chances are you have seen the classic sequence with Charlie Brown, who shouts out to the world, "I love all mankind," and then in the next frame says in a quiet tone, "It's people I can't stand." It is true that getting along with people takes some doing, but unless you are prepared to live the life of a hermit, there is no alternative—you must learn to live with people with a modicum of friendliness and harmony.

The common excuse at this point is "Oh, I have no trouble

getting along with people, as long as I can select the people with whom I have to work and associate." You don't always have that choice, and anyway, it leads to the kind of discrimination that the world can no longer tolerate. Happy relationships in life depend not so much on finding the right person as upon *being* the right person. Getting along with people is only 2 percent the kind of persons they are, and 98 percent the way you react to the kind of people they are. Our resistance to people has little to do with them and everything to do with our fears, our feelings of insecurity, our prejudices.

Here is a little exercise that will help you to see some tendencies within your own nature. Everyone in the world, as far as you are concerned, must fit into one of five classes: enemies, strangers, rivals, friends, teammates. Try this rather painful exercise: Suppose you have a sorting bin. Where are you going to put people—all people—those in your office, in your home, your neighborhood, those you pass on the street, and those who are on the other side of the world? You may discover a little evidence of paranoia as you put too many people in the "enemy" class. And you may find some schizophrenia also as you put too many people in the "stranger" class. As you do this difficult sorting out, you will discover that your problem is not so much the other persons (the 2 percent), but your feelings about them (the 98 percent).

We have been reared in the tradition that all persons are created equal, but this does not mean that all are equal in the same sense that two sticks are equal. Society is a living organism, not a heap of sand. Each person is unique and individual. Most of the problems of getting along with people come from the fact that we have felt that if people are equal they must conform to a common standard. So we use terms such as "normal," "mature," "decent." We call certain persons immature, or we define their behavior as abnormal or indecent, expecting them to conform to what we believe is normal or mature or decent. We see people in the light of what we believe they should be instead of as they are. Of course, it is not easy to see people in this way, in view of the obvious faults they have. But then, what are we trying to do, look for faults in others, or try to get along with them?

We may go so far as to blame the faults in others as the reason we can't get along with them; but this simply evidences our own inability to relate, to love, to trust, and be friendly. We are more often using the faults of others to justify our inability or unwillingness to relate to them freely. And there is no point in trying to change other people so you can get along better with them. You can only change *you*: alter your attitudes, let go of your resistance. Actually, you do seem in this way to change the other, because you change the level at which you relate to and draw from that person.

It is a great cosmic truth that within each of us is the unborn possibility of limitless experience and ours is the privilege of giving birth to it. There is enough energy of love in us to embrace all people, even the most disturbing and unruly person. If you are willing to turn on the light, the chances are excellent that you will avoid conflicts and achieve a peaceful, if not a friendly relationship. You *can* get along with all people— the power to do so is within you.

25. The Opportunity of Marriage

I have a minister friend who says that the most disturbing thing in his ministry is the discovery of how rare it is to sign a marriage license for a couple who have not been married at least once before. Certainly the divorce rate today is something to be concerned about.

British poet T. S. Eliot characterizes the plight of so many marriages with devastating simplicity in this line from *The Cocktail Party*:

> They do not repine;
> Are contented with the morning that separates
> And with the evening that brings together
> For casual talks before the fire;
> Two people who know they do not understand each other,
> Breeding children whom they do not understand
> And who will never understand them.

We often hear the statement, "This or that marriage failed." But it is not marriage that fails. It is people who fail. All marriage ever does is show people up. No real, healthy adjustment can be made in marriage until the individuals involved realize that as individuals they have a responsibility to improve upon the person they presented themselves as being in the beginning of their relationship.

It seems to me that the first crisis of marriage comes when two people look at each other through the foggy glass of emotional love and say, "He (or she) is just about the most perfect creature ever born." In the first place, people are not perfect. The fact that two people are drawn to one another is evidence of instability; of each one seeking stability and security and strength through uniting with another.

Each of us has the potential of being that "most perfect creature ever born." And perhaps that is what love is—the ability to see prophetically, to see one another as we can be. This, coupled with the will to roll up our sleeves and help the other person to fulfill that potential. But this means that marriage is not walking through the festive archway to live happily ever after. It is the open door into a workshop of human growth and development.

Happiness in marriage is not a bequest, but a conquest. It is earned by effort and discipline and patience and understanding. And the blessings of marriage may come in the form of challenges. Sometimes challenges are the very thing we need to meet to spur us on to growth and development as individuals. Socrates was once asked by a young man whether he should marry. The wise one replied, "Marry by all means. If you get a good wife you will be happy. If you get a poor wife, you will become a philosopher and that is good for any man." This may seem small comfort when a home is disrupted by differences of opinion and temperament. But let us be humble enough to consider the possibility that marriage is a divine process by which two people are brought together who have the character and consciousness to be the right challenge and the right influence in helping each other to unfold their inner potential. And then let us be unselfish enough to get our thoughts away from ourselves long enough to look for the ways in which we can be more understanding, more patient, and more downright helpful to this person with whom we share such a great investment of feelings, of materials things, and of years of our life.

I think it was Goethe who said, "Marriage is not a goal in itself, but an opportunity to mature."

26. The Hunger for Appreciation

We have been told that hunger is the number one problem in the world, and that there are millions of people who have never known what it was to go to bed at night without pangs of hunger. But did you know that the most unsatisfied hunger in the world is the hunger to be appreciated? We don't have to go to Africa or India to find victims. We can probably find them in your office and perhaps even in your home.

Often we say of a person who is moody or rebellious or critical or sullen, "What's eating him?" The truth is he is eating his heart out for lack of appreciation. This is a very real need in the lives of everyone, including you.

Dr. William James had a long and protracted illness. A friend sent him a potted azalea with a few words of appreciation. In acknowledging the gift, the distinguished philosopher-psychologist said it had reminded him of an omission of which he was guilty in writing his book on psychology. He found that he had omitted from his textbook the deepest quality of human nature—the craving to be appreciated.

I suspect that Dr. James is not the only one who has been guilty of such an omission. Sometimes a word or even a smile of appreciation for the obscure little acts of generosity and kindness on the part of people whose lives touch ours would ignite the spark of joy within those whose lives are otherwise lifeless and sad.

How often married couples take each other's virtues for granted and concentrate on each other's shortcomings! How much better to look for the good in one another and to say nice things about each other when the opportunity arises. Business executives, who know that warm expressions of approval and praise make for better relationships in the business world, often forget to apply the same practice at home. Wives who see that fault-finding rarely accomplishes anything in their jobs and social activities forget that it is equally self-defeating with their husbands. Sometimes the only real problem with problem children is the hunger for praise and appreciation, a desperate need for love and moral support.

I would like to suggest an experiment. For just one full working day, see how many commendable things you can observe in people, things they do for you—or wisely refrain from doing—or things they do for others, or good qualities they reveal that are the result of obvious self-discipline. If the service is good in the restaurant or if the newsboy is particularly pleasant or businesslike, act on the impulse to express your appreciation. You see, it isn't necessarily that we don't think about it. But too often we think about it but fail to express it, and someone who might be fed immeasurably by our words of praise continues to suffer the hunger for appreciation. Say those nice things, don't merely think them! Too much good intention in this life is buried in silence.

You will be amazed at the good you will find in people if you go looking for it. And the interesting part of it is this—when we appreciate and acknowledge things that are worthwhile in others, that appreciation and understanding will be reflected in the advancement of those things worthwhile in us.

"I am a little thing with a big meaning. I unlock doors, open hearts, dispel prejudices. I create friendships and goodwill. Everybody loves me. I cost nothing. I am appreciation."

27. Be an Ordinary Person

I recently heard someone exclaim, in reference to a person of decency and largeness of spirit, "What an extraordinary person!" Though I shared the feeling of admiration, I found myself wondering, "Is he really extraordinary? Or is he an evidence of the truly ordinary?"

We have tended to think of "ordinary" as below average, somewhat inferior. Actually, the word *ordinary* is more accurately defined as "normal, natural." Perhaps we have been influenced by Hollywood's use of superlatives. When movies are referred to as "superior... colossal ... stupendous," who wants to see an "ordinary" one? For that matter, who wants to be an "ordinary" person?

The person who is confident yet humble, loving yet wise, successful yet still interested in others is usually referred to as an "extraordinary" human being. But it seems to me that this downgrades the race as a whole. It implies that we are an inferior product which only occasionally turns out well. This has been the traditional religious view, but it certainly isn't my view.

If ever there was a person who qualified for the "extraordinary" label it would be the man Jesus. Yet he always rejected such accolades. "Why callest thou me good?" he asked. "All that I do you can do too, if you have faith." Jesus glorified the common man, implying that common to all persons is a God-potential for all-sufficiency. It follows that he who releases this potential is the normal person, the ordinary person. The extraordinary person is one who frustrates his God-potential and thus fails to express the divinely natural qualities of love and justice and wisdom.

Consider the "common cold." It is never natural to have a cold or any kind of sickness. For the human organism, a cold is an unusual thing, an abnormal thing, an "extraordinary" thing, if you will. If a person were truly and wholly himself all the time, if he were what he is meant to be, he would never be sick.

Because we have accepted the cold as "common," we call those very few people who *never* have a cold extraordinary. In point of fact, they are ordinary, normal, and natural, while the millions who get the colds are abnormal, unnatural, and "extraordinary." It is not a matter of numbers or statistics, but of departure from a norm. Sickness is always abnormal. The body is always biased on the side of health. It is never natural to be sick, and even the medical report of "death by natural causes" is no longer considered accurate.

Too often we lose sight of the fact that the moral and psychic and emotional norm for humans is not to express selfishness, hatred, or destructive tendencies. When we act in all the anti-social ways that we have come to accept as common in our urban society, we must remind ourselves that these ways are *not* the norm; they are abnormal, unnatural, extraordinary.

So when we see those occasional evidences of graciousness, honesty, integrity, and love, they represent what we all ought to be; what we are meant to be and *can* be. They represent the natural human state, somehow uncontaminated by the infections of negativity that plague so much of society.

It is vital to our healthy-mindedness to believe in the norm of goodness, to have faith in the inherent goodness in people, to know that all the vanities and lusts and piques are simply the frustration of this basic goodness. The goal of every person should be to erase these frustrations. And when one person succeeds, even in a small way, he ennobles us all. He is not the extraordinary person but the ordinary one, the normal one. For he has demonstrated true human nature.

28. The Art of Listening

I would like to challenge you to think a little bit about the "art of listening." Editor and author Bennet Cerf has said, "Listening is a lost art. Nobody listens any more."

We think of the ear when we use the word "listening"—but did you know that you really listen with your mind? To listen connotes an inward response to an outward stimulus, a sensitivity to vibration. And vibration is everywhere. We can and ultimately must cultivate the ability to hear and heed the message of the cosmic intelligence within us and in the world around us. Shakespeare points to this in *As You Like It* when he talks of finding "tongues in trees, books in the running brooks, Sermons in stones, and good in every thing."

American philosopher William James said, "If we could splice the outer extremities of our optic nerves to our ears, and those of our auditory nerves to our eyes, we should hear the lightning and see the thunder, see the symphony and hear the conductor's movements." In other words, the kind of impressions we receive from the world about us depends for each of us simply upon how we happen to be put together, upon our individual mental makeup.

Perhaps you recall the fable of the three blind men and the elephant. To the man who caught hold of the elephant's leg, the elephant was like a tree. To the man who felt his side, the elephant was like a wall. To the one who seized his tail, the elephant was like a rope. The world is to each one of us the work of our own perception, with no two perceptions quite alike.

You are like a radio receiving station. Every moment thousands of impressions are reaching you. You can tune in on whatever you like. You may listen to the beauty of nature or you may fix your attention upon the filth of a city street. You may listen to joy or sorrow, success or failure, optimism or fear. Each of us is born with the equipment to hear, but we must cultivate the ability to hear rightly, to listen selectively.

Actually, while hearing is in the realm of the senses, true listening is extrasensory in nature—it is feeling; it is consciousness. A Beethoven symphony may be playing. All within the range of the sound hear the music, but by no means do all get the message. English poet Elizabeth Barrett Browning must have felt this when she wrote:

> Earth's crammed with heaven
> And every common bush afire with God;
> And only he who sees takes off his shoes—
> The rest sit round it and pluck blackberries.

Cultivate the habit of listening. It must begin with a polite attentiveness to people who are speaking. How often conversation is simply a relay of talking, with little or no actual listening. One man suggests this prayer: "God give me the patience to listen until the other fellow tells half of what he believes before I start in to tell him all I know."

When we form the habit of listening creatively, we become receptive to the higher vibrations of a cosmic voice from which all intelligence springs. It is absolutely amazing—the things we can do when we walk and work under the guidance of the "still small voice within us." Our guidance may not come with a dramatic experience like Moses and the burning bush, but come it will if we listen. As the poet says, "There is guidance for everyone, and by lowly listening we shall hear the right word." Life can be dynamic and effective and decisive and confident when we develop the art of listening.

29.   How to Give and Receive Criticism

Let's think about criticism. The English poet Samuel Taylor Coleridge once said, "Experience informs us that the first defense of weak minds is to recriminate." That is pretty stern stuff, isn't it? The psychologist will tell you that the tendency toward criticism comes from a sense of inferiority. Carping at another's weaknesses gives you a feeling of strength. It is a subconscious attempt to cut the other person down to your size. If we can honestly face up to the reasons why we criticize others, we will come to understand why others criticize us.

People reveal much about themselves in criticizing others, and you tell about yourself in your reaction to criticism. What another says or does—even to you—is that person's business; but your reaction to what is said or done—your resistance, anger, or feeling of hurt—that is your business. The other person may say some unkind things, and may even be intent on picking you apart, but why should you let that determine how you are going to act?

If it is difficult for you to meet criticism, you have a problem. It is not just that you have a thin skin. It is that you have a need for development and your defensiveness to criticism is your awareness of the need to grow as a person. It is important that you face up to this. Tell yourself, "I want to grow. I want to be more. I want to discover everything I can about myself that will help me to make progress as a person, so I welcome this criticism." In the face of any direct or implied criticism, ask yourself, "How can I benefit from this?" I have a simple slogan that works wonders for me: *Do your best, and leave the rest.* If the critic points out something that shows a way to better your best, then give thanks for it. No matter what motivated the criticism, you can receive great benefit from it. Silently or openly, say "Thank you for your help." If, on the other hand, the act of criticism simply shows a weakness on the part of the person making the criticism, then leave the rest, and let it go. Literally drop it in the wastebasket. Your positive response to what appears to be negative things can and often does turn them into assets. As it has been said, "Even a kick in the pants is a boost, if you are headed in the right direction."

Now, what about your criticism of others? Should we never criticize? Are we to keep still when we know something is wrong? I know someone who keeps on his desk a stone with the word "first" painted on it in red letters. Remember the Bible story, "He that is without sin may throw the first stone." So this is the "first stone" that the man refuses to throw. It is a good reminder, for throwing stones is a habit with many of us. Somebody says something we do not like and, before we think, we heave that stone. We may regret it immediately, but by then the damage is done. There *are* times, of course, when constructive criticism needs to be offered. As a friend, or parent, or teacher, or employer, it is a duty to help the person to make needed adjustments in character or performance. A good rule is to reflect on the question: It is true, is it kind, is it needful? Then, if the answer is yes, how can I say it in the most tactful and loving way?

The word "criticism," coined by Aristotle, originally meant "looking for the good." This is the highest form of criticism: looking for the good in people, and if you receive criticism from others, determining that it will find the good in you. Praise is the most effective technique in constructive criticism you can employ. Find something to praise in people who need help, and they will begin to reveal more of their best; condemn them for their mistakes and they will reveal more of their worst. Goethe once said: "If we take people as they are we make them worse. If we treat them as if they were what they should be, we make them what they can be."

Let your criticism take a new high level—look for the good in all persons, and determine that you will react to all persons from the good in yourself. Try it—it will work for you.

30. The Grace of Receiving

We often hear it said, "It is more blessed to give than to receive." But I wonder if we do not tend to forget the other side of the coin, that for everyone that gives there must also be someone big enough to receive. And it takes a really big person to receive a gift without feeling the burden of obligation.

A few years ago I was on an automobile trip across the country. I was passing through a town where an old army friend of mine lived, so I decided to stop in and surprise him. I took a carefully selected gift to his young daughter. After our visit I presented the gift, but the parents would not allow the child to accept it. They made such a fuss about it that I could see that they were going to be quite hurt if I insisted. So, I sheepishly walked away with the gift still in my possession.

It was a long trip and I had time to think about this experience. First of all, I decided that I did not want this little episode to stand in the way of our friendship. And next, I began to realize that their reaction was a very common one and that it was caused by the fear of being under obligation, of having to do something in return.

I remembered a time when a man, whom I knew to be struggling with alcoholism, had volunteered to do some work around my yard. He worked hard all day. I recall the joy in his face. It seemed as if he were experiencing something transcendent. When he was ready to leave in the evening he thanked me for letting him work. I felt that he should have some payment, for he was out of work. Though he objected, I pressed some money into his hand. The look on his face I will always remember. It was as if I had taken all the props from under him. I later discovered he had gone right into another "lost weekend." I had failed him by denying him the opportunity to regain his self-respect.

Once I was driving down town with a friend, and we saw someone we knew standing on the corner waiting for the bus. We stopped and invited her to ride with us. When we arrived at her destination she thanked me and dropped a quarter on the front seat, and before I could object she was gone. I suddenly felt cheap about my boy scout deed. The friend with me said, "She did not mean that as an insult. She is a fine woman, but oh so independent! She insists upon paying her own way through life. She won't let anyone give her anything."

We all know many people like that, don't we? They go blithely on their way through life, deluding themselves that they are gracious and open; when in reality they are extremely selfish individuals. They do not realize it, of course, but every time they refuse to allow someone to do something for them, they are selfishly refusing that person the opportunity to realize the joy and the blessing of giving.

Unfortunate indeed is this resistance to being under obligation. The struggle to "get even" goes on continuously with most of us. I invite you over to my house for dinner; you must immediately invite me. I buy your lunch; you must buy mine. I send you a Christmas card; and immediately my name goes on your card list for next year (and you probably run out and buy a late card which you send off air mail this year). Little do we know what we are doing—it is a selfish race to see who can get ahead of the other in being the most generous person. How much better to know that it is just as important to be a good receiver as a good giver. Sometimes the greatest thing you can do for others is to let them do something for you.

31. Praise

I once knew a man whose name wouldn't mean much to you, but whose way of life should. He traveled a great deal through the country in the course of his business. But no matter where he went or what mission he was on, he never forgot the business of human relations; the matter of trying to give people a boost instead of a kick.

He was hurrying through a railroad station one day when he passed a crippled beggar who was sitting with his hat at the ready to receive coins and selling pencils. On impulse he dropped a coin in the hat and hurried on his way. Suddenly, after walking on a short distance, he stopped short, pondered a moment, and then turned back to the beggar. He said, "I want to apologize to you. I treated you like a beggar, when in fact you are a merchant." He reached down and took one of the pencils and turned to continue on his way.

Several years later he happened to be passing through this same station. A voice called him, "Hey mister!" It was the attendant of a busy newsstand. "You don't remember me, do you; but I sure remember you. A few years ago you told me I was a merchant and not a beggar. You were the first person who had ever treated me as an equal. I really was a beggar, but you helped me to see that I could live a normal life and make a living for myself. I started selling newspapers and now I have this newsstand which is doing more business than any stand in the station. Thanks to you."

You never really know how far-reaching is the effect or influence of your words and actions on the lives of another. Shakespeare wrote in *The Merchant of Venice*: "How far that little candle throws his beams! So shines a good deed in a naughty world!"

The key to this kind of goodness is *praise*. We all know from sad experience how criticism and condemnation can cut you down. And we all know how good we feel when someone gives us a word of praise. When you praise, you raise the person to a higher level of thinking, to better spirits, to a renewed determination to press on. Praise is a miracle worker. We should use it more often.

A retired teacher says that she once had a young boy in her class who was completely incorrigible. She says that she came very close to giving up her work as a teacher because of him. One day he came to school with a clean shirt. His hands were still dirty and his pants torn, but he had a clean shirt. She praised him for it. That very afternoon he returned with a tattered tie on his shirt. She praised him for the tie. The next day he had new shoelaces. She passed the word around to the other teachers to praise him. In time this young lad was transformed. He not only became an excellent student, but later he became the president of a large midwestern university. Such is the power of praise.

Praise is a sort of spiritual vitamin. People need some of it to be emotionally healthy, to be their best and do their best. It is a precious plus in life. Like the little cake of yeast that magically leavens the lump of dough, a little praise can transform our whole lives.

Praise can bring harmony to the home and efficiency to an office. Praise can boost sagging spirits and increase talents and abilities—it sounds almost like the claims of one of our miracle drugs. Praise is not found in a bottle, however, but in ourselves. Everyone can give praise, and everyone should. All of us hunger for a word of praise. Mark Twain once said, "I can live for two months on a good compliment."

Remember, while there is much in the course of our days that tends to pulls us down, to discourage and defeat us, praise is that which lifts us up. Praise serves to raise. Try it. The miracle is that it is helpful alike to giver and to receiver.

IV. Living Healthfully

32. The Key to Mental Health

In America we have one of the highest standards of living in the world. Americans have greater opportunities, more freedoms, less poverty than any other people in the world. And yet, the number of cases of ulcers has never been higher, psychiatrists' couches are occupied constantly by the frustrated and unsatisfied, and mental illness is growing at such a rate that it is estimated that one out of every ten Americans born this year will spend some part of his life under care for mental illness! Why?

Perhaps the main reason is that in one way or another people feel inadequate for life. Life seems to be too much for them, and their mental illness is an unconscious means of escape from reality. The sad part of it all is that most of those who go to pieces are defeated not because they are actually inadequate for the strain of living, but because they think they are. It is our fear of inadequacy, our fear of failure, that causes the strain and the ultimate breakdown.

I remember a time in college when I was singing a solo for a student assembly. The number I had been asked to sing had a high B-flat in it, and my uncertain tenor voice could barely manage an A-flat. Occasionally I could reach for the vicinity of an A-natural, but a B-flat would cause me to break down every time. I had arranged with my accompanist to transpose the song into a lower key that would only require an A-flat. The problem was that the girl forgot, so I sang the number through, handling the B-flat with ease, and thinking I was only singing the A-flat. When I discovered what had happened I was chagrined, and then enriched with a great lesson: I realized that my crackups on the B-flat were not due to inadequacy but to the fear of inadequacy.

In the same way, people go to pieces not so much because they are inadequate as because they are afraid they are inadequate. The problem, fundamentally, is one of faith—whether you are singing or living. You can handle the challenges of your life if you believe you have the capacity to meet them.

Thus we see that common, ordinary faith is the key to mental health. Josiah Royce of Harvard University said in his book *The Religious Aspect of Philosophy*, "Faith is the soul's insight or discovery of some reality that will enable a man to stand anything that may happen to him."

Katherine Mansfield had this quality of faith through the lonely, pain-wracked days she struggled against tuberculosis. She went on writing lovely poetry. Her journal records a moving struggle as she grew through rebellion to acceptance to triumph. Finally she wrote, "I feel happy—deep down. All is well." She sang her way to the end, knowing she could stand anything.

The great challenge for Americans, then, seems to be the need, despite our split-level homes, gadget-lined kitchens, and well-cushioned lives, to develop a firm faith to live by—faith in ourselves, and faith in something greater than ourselves, which is at the same time ever within ourselves.

No matter who you are or what your particular circumstances may be, you are adequate for anything that can happen to you if you have linked your life by faith to the limitless resources of the Infinite.

33. Your Fountain of Youth

One of the greatest untruths that has relentlessly been foisted upon generation after generation is that "from the day of your birth you begin to die." This may appear to be poetic insight, but it is just not true.

One man was talking about his octogenarian father recently. He said, "There's nothing exactly wrong with him. Just worn out, I guess. After all, he's past eighty." But the human body does not operate according to a mechanical timetable. The famous Italian conductor Toscanini, at the age of nearly ninety years, was said by music lovers to still retain superb ability and technique. Why is it that some persons look and act old at fifty while others are strong and active at eighty? It has been said that decrepitude, senility, and the other characteristics of old age are brought on more often by mental attitudes than by the passing of years, and that fear, doubt, and worry produce more sagging bodies and lagging minds than we realize. In this respect, old Solomon was certainly right when he said, "As he thinketh within himself, so is he."

Several years ago there was a black man named Sam, who had lived in the neighborhood as long as anyone could remember. When asked about his age he had one answer: he was eighty-four. He kept busy cutting grass, shoveling snow, and doing other odd jobs around the neighborhood. He often laughed and told friends he would work until he was a hundred, and then retire.

One day Sam received a box from North Carolina, and a letter telling him of a brother's death. The box contained some of his brother's belongings, and among them was a worn Bible, its pages yellow with age. On one of the fly-leaves was recorded: "Samuel—born to Bertha and Jacob"—and the date, indicating that Sam was actually well past one hundred years of age.

When it was explained to him, he blinked his eyes and said, "Guess I'm a pretty old man." The way Sam slowed down after that was positively amazing. Previously his posture had been good and his mind keen, but now he began to fail rapidly. He was permitted to live in his little house without paying rent, and the neighbors kept him supplied with food, but he only lived a little over a year. And I sometimes wonder just how long Sam might have lived had he not learned his true birthdate.

To keep from growing old, we of course do not have to avoid knowing the number of years we have lived, though it is certain that some of us put all too much emphasis on birthdays. Most important is that we do not let this knowledge influence our mental attitude or our actions. You are really as young as you think.

Reliable statistics show that the average normal child born in the United States during the Civil War was expected to live less than forty years. The average young man of twenty-five today is expected to reach seventy-five or over. Who can say that in the next century it will not be quite common for men and women to live a hundred and fifty years?

It is said that when Ponce de León returned to Spain after his fruitless search for the Fountain of Youth he said to a friend, "I have indeed been a fool. After journeying so far in search of the Fountain of Youth, I return home and find that it is right here inside me. It was here all the time. Yes, my friend," he said, "the Fountain of Youth is within your own heart."

34. The Prince and the Statue

Perhaps you have heard the story of the woman who had been impressed with the concept that the mother's thoughts during pregnancy would have a definite prenatal influence upon the child. Hoping to influence her child with brilliance she decided to spend time reading classic literature. She read the book *David Copperfield,* and her child turned out to be a little Dickens!

There is a great deal of truth, however, in the matter of the influence upon our lives of the things we visualize. The *Journal of Education* some years ago carried a story entitled "The Prince and the Statue" that brought this matter into sharp focus:

There was once a prince who had a crooked back. He could never stand up straight like even the lowest of his subjects. Because he was a very proud prince his crooked back caused him a great deal of mental suffering. One day he called before him the most skillful sculptor in his kingdom and said to him: 'Make me a noble statue of myself, true to my likeness in every detail with this exception—make this statue with a straight back. I wish to see myself as I might have been.'

For long months the sculptor worked hewing the marble carefully into the likeness of the prince, and at last the work was done. The prince said, 'Place it in a secret nook in the palace garden where only I shall see it.' The statue was placed as the prince ordered, and promptly forgotten by the world, but every morning and every noon and every evening the prince stole quietly away to where it stood and looked long upon it, noting the straight back and the uplifted head and the noble brow. And each time he gazed, something seemed to go out of the statue and into him, tingling in his blood and throbbing in his heart.

The days passed into months and the months into years; then strange rumors began to spread throughout the land. Said one, 'The prince's back is no longer crooked or my eyes deceive me.' Said another, 'The prince is more noble-looking or my eyes deceive me.' Said another, 'Our prince has the high look of a mighty man,' and these rumors came to the prince, and he listened with a queer smile. Then he went out into the garden to where the statue stood and, behold, it was just as the people said, his back had become as straight as the statue's, his head had the same noble bearing; he was, in fact, the noble man his statue proclaimed him to be.

A strange story, to be sure! But don't toss it off too lightly. It is generally accepted that the environment in which we live has a pronounced effect upon our character and the development of our mind. When we recognize the amazing influence the mind has on the body, there may be more truth than fiction in the idea that if we fix our attention upon a saint we will become a saint, or if we idealize an athlete we might become an athlete. And it is but one more giant step to the concept that if we fix our attention upon the expression of perfect health, that we may realize that perfection in the organs and tissues and functions of our bodies.

Twenty-five hundred years ago, in the Golden Age of Athens, the people were surrounded by beautiful statues of perfect human specimens so that mothers might give birth to perfect babies and men would develop perfect bodies. The Greeks had a word for it!

35. When the Heat's On

"Everybody talks about the weather but nobody does anything about it." That is a statement widely attributed to Mark Twain, though it is likely that it was first stated by an English author. But whoever said it first, I have come to the conclusion that he or she was wrong. We all do something about the weather—we decide whether to resist it or make the best of it.

On an extremely hot day last summer when everyone was talking about the weather, I noticed an old newspaper vendor on the corner who had to stand out in the sun all day and yet looked comparatively cool. I asked him, "What's your secret?" He replied, "Oh, I don't have any secret. I'm philosophic about it. I figgers it can't last forever." Here is a man who has done something about the weather; he has decided not to worry about it or resist it.

In times of peace and harmony it is quite possible to live fairly happily and comfortably without having much of a philosophy of life, for one can just drift with the tide of human affairs. But "when the heat's on," when the weather is unbearably hot or uncomfortably cold, when world affairs or personal affairs become awkward and troublesome, we find that in order to keep from being consumed by experiences, we must develop some sort of philosophy.

Even the negative philosophy, "There's nothing you can do about it so you might as well grin and bear it," has its positive effect. It is a well-established truth that the real discomfort brought about by circumstances, including warm weather, is in our resistance to them and our resentful attitude toward them.

The body of man is equipped with a wonderful air conditioner that enables us to live quite comfortably in extreme heat if we observe a few rules: drink plenty of water, wear comfortable clothing, and avoid overexertion. The mind of man is also equipped with a marvelous air conditioner through its intuitive forces. If we take time for solitude and meditation, a limitless stream of new and dynamic ideas flows freely into and through us.

When the great Japanese-Christian leader Kagawa visited in Washington, a young minister volunteered to act as his chauffeur. The first day the minister drove Kagawa around he was amazed that such a seemingly frail, older man could carry out such an active schedule and still appear fresh. On the second day he was asked to meet Kagawa at 5:00 A.M. and take him to the Tidal Basin. There he discovered the key to the man's serenity and strength of spirit. For over an hour Kagawa sat relaxed and perfectly still on a bench. Apparently he was looking at the rising sun and the play of light as it turned from pink to white on the Jefferson Memorial. Here the great man talked with his God, read his Bible, and charged himself with the peace and power and poise of the Almighty. Then he took up the day's crowded schedule with a glow on his face and a spring in his step. It was a very hot day but he seemed completely unconcerned about it.

When the heat's on—literally and figuratively—you can do something about it. Keep inwardly calm and cool and take time to be still in mind and body, to establish the important contact with the life force and the mind stream. Don't let yourself think about or talk about either the weather or stormy problems of life. Instead think about the marvelous mental and physical air conditioner with which you have been equipped. You might even want to declare affirmatively about the summer heat, as many have so successfully done: "I agree with the weather and the weather agrees with me."

36. How to Avoid Middle-Age Letdown

It has been said that "life begins at forty." This was literally true in pre-Communist China, where traditionally a person was not accepted as a mature adult until the fortieth birthday. Up to that time one was unable to speak one's mind in the presence of elders. There, in a very real sense, life began at forty.

For most of us, however, age forty is a critical time in life. It is either the entrance into or is already within that period known as "middle age." It is difficult to define the term "middle age," simply because age is more psychological than physiological. More relevant to age than our birthdays are our interests, our enthusiasm, and our mental health.

When is a person young or old? Often it may be a question of occupation. President Kennedy, in his mid-forties, was considered an extremely young President. A movie actress at his age would be considered beyond her peak. A baseball player at this age would be thought extremely old. At age fifty a corporation executive is considered young, but a coal miner is old at fifty.

Essentially, "middle age" refers to the period during which a psychological letdown comes to many of us. During the early years of our lives we are preoccupied with growing up, completing our education, raising a family, and getting the children educated. Suddenly the job is through or near completion. We begin to struggle with the question, "Where do we go from here?" We begin to think too much about ourselves—our health, our security, our appearance. We begin to hunt for symptoms. We think of checkups and breakdowns. We quake over every palpitation of the heart, and every shortness of breath. And we often do some rather weird things to try to prove to ourselves that we are still attractive and virile.

This is a time when we need some straight talk. Middle age is not the beginning of the end, but the end of the beginning. So we can't still dance all night or keep up with our sons in touch football! Why should we? If we have lost anything at this stage of life, it is the things we can well do without. It is a time when we should know ourselves better, when our childish aspirations have settled into mature goals.

If there is such a thing as middle age, it should be a time of transition, not to old age, but to a time of new and exciting purpose. We need to get our second wind. And this doesn't mean trying to recreate the appearance of a teenage body. All too many people at this time of life are driven to fantastic extremes in trying to hold on to what they think is lost, using every possible wrinkle they can think of to get rid of wrinkles, bulges, sags, and grey hairs.

Let's face it, getting your face lifted fools no one, and it certainly doesn't change the person inside. The great need is to get your *faith* lifted, your enthusiasm rekindled, your zest for living increased. The formula is really quite simple: Concentrate on that part of you that is ever new—your mind. Keep your mind awake and you'll stay young all over. These are exciting times—frightening, too, perhaps—but exciting. Send your mind back to school. Cultivate an enthusiasm for knowledge, for mental and spiritual expansion. Refuse to think of yourself as old or to see yourself settling down into aging gracefully. Declare affirmatively that you are the kind of vital, creative, enthusiastic, and happy person you want to be.

37. How to Get Out of Your Shell

Life is for living, not for existing, making do, getting old, and dying. How much confusion there is about this thing called life! Instead of moving through life with romance and the spirit of adventure, most persons crawl through their days as if they believed themselves to be mechanical toys winding down.

The thing that makes the difference between youth and age is the attitude with which we face our daily challenges to growth. Note how spontaneously the child deals with life. Moving from one thing to another without worrying whether past failures will affect future experiences, without worrying about what others may say or think, the child simply moves, acts—lives.

How sad that we progressively lose the spontaneity of life, doing all that we do for reasons other than our own free will. We become "other-directed." In the process, we lose the spirit of adventure in life. Work degenerates into dreary monotony. Marriage, which began with such joy and enthusiasm, becomes commonplace in the steady round of day-by-day living. The hopes and ambitions that once stirred us become lifeless. Far horizons no longer beckon. The joy of life flees, leaving our days hollow and our labors meaningless.

It is frightening to observe how we progressively narrow the scope of our lives with what we call "maturity." We settle on a very few interests, select a small number of people with whom to associate, and develop set ways of doing things. We settle on a religion and a political belief, not so much by conviction as to "save us from the vexation of thinking."

We progressively enclose ourselves in a shell—often the shell of self-deprecation. We tend to think of life in terms of what we know we cannot do: "I know myself pretty well after all the years. I know my weaknesses." But do you also know your strengths? Weaknesses are simply limiting shells that enclose greater potentialities. If we focus on weaknesses, we begin to think of life on the wane: it spends our substance, exhausts our ideas, consumes our time, depletes our energy—as the "years dwindle down." And "in the wisdom of the world which is foolishness with God," we place emphasis on caution and conservation and security.

This leads to the trap of materiality, where we become more concerned with *having* money than with *enjoying* it. We become possessed by the very things we count as our possessions. We try to possess life rather than letting it live us. How important, when we have gone as far as we can go in any project, and when we have done all we feel we can do, to let go and walk on! Life is an ongoing experience. We act as if we believed that every experience is a matter of life and death. We must "master the problem, overcome the challenge, succeed at the project!" But why? More important than succeeding is growing, learning, and getting the experience of transcendence.

We get too hung up on the desire for success, and our feelings of guilt over failure. In the "success syndrome," anything less than the very top person on the totem pole is a failure. Thus most of us, albeit unconsciously, have accepted labels of "failure," "incompetent," "inadequate." The truth is: you are not really a success or a failure. You are simply *you*! The real significance of your life is not how high you have climbed or how much you have amassed, but how you have gotten yourself together in consciousness, how you have related to reality all along the way.

Occasionally, some sudden or even tragic change breaks the stark pattern of our lives and reveals how much we had been caught in the comfortable web we had woven around ourselves. How often, in wars or depressions, have people been forced to break the pattern of their lives, and in so doing have discovered resources within themselves they had not known to exist. But the sad thing is that so many persons are content to live half a life.

Education has always been the finest way to challenge people to break out of their shells. Education is not simply a classroom and a teacher, however. The most enriching classroom is the world around us. We need to challenge ourselves with the words of the old hymn: "Open my eyes that I may see, . . . open my ears that I may hear, ... open my heart that I may feel."

The opportunities for growth through learning are everywhere, but you must become like a little child and invest yourself despite the risks of failure. There is no happiness except through reaching. It is only by reaching that you keep young. No one really *grows* old; when someone stops reaching for the highest, he is old. But don't misunderstand: this highest is not the high place on the totem pole but the undeveloped awareness by which you contemplate things from the highest point of view.

Josh Billings says, "It is not only the most difficult thing to know oneself, but the most inconvenient one, too." We employ a variety of clever devices for running away from ourselves. We keep ourselves too busy, fill our lives with diversions, stuff our heads with knowledge, and cover as much ground as possible— so that we have no time to probe the wonderful world within and around us. Thus we are prisoners of our own making.

When the chick awakens to the fact that it is cramped inside the egg, it is a most natural thing to peck its way out. Suddenly, it is in a wonderful world of worms and seeds and undreamed of adventures. Although it takes the chick only a few minutes to break its shell, you may find it a little more difficult to break your shell of inadequacy and fear and self-limitation. But, as with the chick, there is a wonderful world awaiting you.

One of the most effective ways of getting the experience of breaking out of the shell routines in life is literally, or figuratively (in a meditation), to "take a walk." Emerson says, "I think it is the best of mankind that goes for a walk." We are not talking about a walk to the store or to Aunt Emma's. Just take a walk in which you spontaneously experience the world around you—and within you. Let the city or the countryside "happen" to you. It will be as in Genesis, "And the Lord looked upon the creation, and it was good!"

Determine that you will break the shell that comprises the ruts and routines of your life, the limiting patterns of thought, the repetitive tendencies of sameness. Open your eyes and see, open your ears and hear, and you will experience yourself and the world around you. You will find new frontiers of discovery and knowledge for the asking. Remember, life is not for existing or making do. Life is for living and growing. Break out of your shell of self-limitation and get on with the joyous business of living.

38. The Quest for Attractiveness

Does it make you feel good when someone compliments you on your appearance? Of course it does. We all have a desire to be attractive to others. To this end we do some strange and peculiar things. We follow style trends to determine what to wear. Many women put in long sessions at the beauty parlor, and we men take care to shave at least once a day and we spend time in selecting just the right necktie.

All around us, wherever we go, are advertisements telling us how we can become beautiful or handsome, how to have a slim figure, broad shoulders, or a schoolgirl complexion. We make tremendous sacrifices in trying to be attractive to others. Many a girl who is nearsighted will endure eyestrain rather than wear glasses, which she thinks will make her less attractive. Many a man will put himself in debt to buy a sporty car that he thinks will enhance his sex appeal. The desire for attractiveness is a wholly serious pursuit.

However, notwithstanding all the great efforts, the expenditure of money, the worrying, the study before mirrors, the consulting of books, doctors, beauticians and astrologers, how many individuals ever attain their goal? In my opinion, very few. Why? Isn't our wonderful modern science able to transform an ugly duckling into a swan?

The answer is simple. Most of us have tried the wrong methods. Beauty is not for sale, and it has never been for sale in all the world's history. All that has been available for a price has been a poor imitation. Genuine beauty that is the wellspring of attractiveness to others is little concerned with purely physical appearance. George Sand, the famous Frenchwoman who adopted a man's name and who is acknowledged to have been one of the world's most attractive women, was so downright homely that British author Thomas Carlyle described her as "horse-faced." But young men fell in love with her when she was seventy.

Think of all the loveable, attractive people you have known.

How many of them were physically glamorous? They may have been even decidedly unlovely from the standpoint of the physical, but you always thought of them as beautiful.

It has been commonly said through the ages that "beauty is only skin deep" and "handsome is as handsome does." Certainly we do not think of someone as attractive when we find selfishness and ignorance. In his book *Psychology in Living,* Wendell White, a University of Minnesota psychologist, points out that "no one sees readily nor long the beauty of an unsympathetic or selfish person. And anyone may find a physical deficiency in an otherwise attractive person overshadowed by his good qualities."

I know a schoolteacher in her forties who is about as beautiful physically as a garden weed. Yet she is a most attractive woman when she speaks to you; then she is transformed into a veritable Helen of Troy. Her warm, rich personality floods over you like a cascade of perfume. She is loved by her students and by everyone she meets.

The secret of genuine, lasting beauty is contained not in the shape of one's nose or the color of one's skin, but within oneself. It is an intangible combination of spiritual and mental qualities that every human being has at his or her command. The next time you want to know how attractive you are, don't rely solely on your mirror, but look within yourself. It is determined by your attitude toward others. If you don't like what you see, get busy and make some inner changes.

39. The Birthday of Your Life

A birthday for most people marks the day of their emergence into life. But what is "life"? It does not begin with birth or end with death. If we can accept the possibility of reincarnation, then a birthday may be the re-emergence of the soul in another physical expression. Can the true birthday of your life be limited to a date on a birth-certificate?

There are some subtle negative implications in the usual practice of birthdays. They set up a crystallized pattern that, because of the emphasis on a fixed date as the point of beginning, makes life a continuous cycle of counting years and anticipating death. Out of this comes many cliches, such as, "For a person of his years he does pretty good." But what is that supposed to mean? That decrepitude is inexorably tied to advancing years?

There is an interesting and significant thought in Job. "If you set your heart aright, ... your life will be brighter than the noonday, ... and you will have confidence, because there is hope" (11:13–18, RSV). At high noon it is difficult to find our way by the sun, for we cannot tell where it rose or where it will set. So "life brighter than noonday" would indicate life without consciousness of length of years, life enriched by the awareness of depths of enthusiasm, wit, and vigor. In this consciousness you will be "like the morning. And you will have confidence, because there is hope."

Don't play the numbers game with age. Length of life is irrelevant. All that ever counts is depth of living. Don't be concerned about when you were born. Just be sure to come alive to each day. What are you doing with the gift of life and the opportunity that is yours to express the creative process? Many a person who celebrates a birthday has little more to celebrate in terms of great moments of livingness. Life is your continuing opportunity to give expression to the creative process. This can be done only by accepting each day as the most important moment of eternity.

The birthday of your life is today! This is your day of birth no matter what the calendar says. This day you opened your eyes to behold a world of need and a world of opportunity. What are you doing about it? What kind of thoughts are you thinking? What goals are you reaching for? What achievements are you making? Some day will you look back on this date as a great moment of your eternal existence?

The author Thomas Carlyle said, "Every day that comes into the world comes like a burst of music, and rings the whole day through, and you will make of it a dance, a dirge, or a life-march as you will."

One man complained, "Oh, when you have lived as long as I have, one day is pretty much the same as the next!" But it is your *birth*day! Or it can be. You are born into the world today.

What are you doing about it? This day holds for you just about anything that you are willing to see in it. It can be as unique and unusual as your creative approach to it. Meet this day and every day with a spirit of joy and enthusiasm and eager antici- pation of the adventure of living.

Your attitude toward your work tells much about your ideals in life. If you say of your work, "Oh, it's a living," then it is not a living at all, but an existence. One woman who delighted in her work as a social worker went out each day into the areas of the economically disadvantaged to work with families in need. Because she knew that these people lived in a veritable hell of existence, she would say facetiously to her family as she left for work each morning, "Well, I'm going out to raise hell today!" And it is very likely, due to her positive and loving attitude, that she brought the birthday of life into the experience of many of her needy charges.

A true birth experience takes place when we actually give birth to something. It is the mother who gives birth to the child, thus the date of a child's birth should be *her* birthday, not the child's. In childbirth a woman participates in the greatest crea- tive act. Actually, we should send a card and a gift to our mother on our birthday, rather than the other way around. And if we want a specific date to commemorate our own birthday, let it be some time when we have actually given birth to something—the launching of an important project, the discovery of a new in- sight, the beginning of a new way of life.

Every person is as old as God and as young as the morning. If you think anything else is true, it is *because* you think it, and *as* you think it. If you downplay the fact of birthdays as the start of the countdown of life, then you may begin to live each day creatively. Each and every day would then become a day of birth into a world to be discovered and experienced.

Every time you experience a new awareness, a new insight, a new discovery in yourself, you give birth to something. You are born again into a new world, and things will never be the same again. Whenever you have any kind of illumination experience, say to yourself "Happy Birthday!" for you are truly "born again." Don't let the date of the happening become a fixation, however. The problem of the "born again" belief in religion is that it is accepted as a once-and-for-all experience of salvation, which is delusion. Salvation is for every day, and on a day-by-day basis.

Rather than sitting around counting birthdays, avail yourself of the opportunity to make each day a time of birth. Then determine that you will make it so by giving birth to something new in your life. Like the social worker, go out and raise a little hell, give expression to the best of your consciousness in trying to make the world a little better place in which to live.

Happy birthday to you! I am not mistaken about your birth date. I am simply giving you a blessing, in the hope that you will give birth to something of yourself today—some act of love or thoughtfulness or appreciation. And remember, every day can be met with the idea, "This is my birthday, my opportunity to deal with the world in a new and creative way."

V. Work and Success

40. Your Possible Dream

In the musical *The Man from La Mancha* there is an inspiring and hopeful song, "To Dream the Impossible Dream." The thing that Cervantes seems to be saying through his Don Quixote is that it is vital to reach, to yearn, to hope, to dream—for a life without dreams is only half a life. Through the ages "reaching for the moon" has been the metaphor for an impossible goal. But in our time someone began seeing it as possible, and now we have a new frontier for exploration and all the impossible dreams of science fiction are becoming increasingly possible in our time.

It is interesting to note that in the splitting of the atom no new power is created, rather a power already present is at long last released. There is a power within you, which, if you could discover and release it, would make you become everything you ever dreamed you could become. Couple this with the fact that the dreams or ideals that are born into your mind have a cosmic origin and you see that your desires and deep aspirations are the prophecies of what you can become. As Emerson says in "Progress of Culture," "no hope so bright but is the beginning of its own fulfillment."

The great tragedy of any life is that these high yearnings have been permitted to deteriorate into impossible dreams. It is absolutely shocking how many people are plodding along at their jobs and in marriages and life situations in conformity to all the things the established society expects of them, but who have given up all hope of betterment, of change, of opportunity, even of love. They have "no hope" and "impossible" written all over their faces. We need to listen to people of action who say, "Impossible is a word to be found only in the directory of fools." When we are faced with those things that seem beyond achieving—wants we cannot cure, sins we cannot master, conflicts we cannot harmonize, we should listen to the vision of American poet Walt Whitman, as he sings: "Oh, while I live, to be the ruler of life, not a slave. To meet life as a powerful conqueror.... And nothing exterior shall ever take command of me."

The measure of your life today is not what you have done but what you are reaching for. The size of a person is always indicated by the depth and breadth of his or her dreams. Of course, there are two kinds of dreams: (1) Wouldn't it be wonderful if ... but of course, it can't be done! and (2) Wouldn't it be wonderful if.... And why not! There must be a way! It can be done, and I'll do it! The only truly "idle dreamer" is one who has no real faith that dreams can be made real.

Remember the story of Pygmalion, who made a statue of marble so beautiful that every woman who saw it envied it. It was so perfect that the sculptor fell in love with it himself, hung it with flowers and jewels, and spent day after day in rapt admiration of it. Finally the gods took pity on him and breathed into it the breath of life.

Dare to dream. If you don't have an expanding vision of your work, your home, your future, then you had better get one. As poet Robert Browning said, "A man's reach should exceed his grasp, else what's a heaven for." It is only by reaching that you challenge yourself to call upon your transcendent potentialities. And don't forget that the real source of happiness and satisfaction in life is not in what you have accomplished or accumulated. It is in what you are living and working for, your vision, your aspirations, your dreams. Thus, when one project or course of your life is complete, you had better dream some new dreams or cast off some old one, or life will suddenly lose its meaning.

The poet Mary Mae Oesch says it in "Dare to Believe":

> Dare to dream! Success awaits
>   Your magic touch. And God creates
> Through you. Fling wide the golden gates
>   To the realm of your heart's desire.

41. Making the Breaks of Life

During World War II, an army officer became lost on the country roads in England. All signposts had been removed in fear of an invasion. Finally he was forced to stop at a farmhouse to ask directions. The youth of whom he inquired scratched his head. He looked down the road one way, then the other, and then said, "Mister, I don't think there's any way to get to London from here!"

There are many people who sit by the side of the road in life, waiting for a break, an opportunity, because they have decided that the only way to get to London, to success, is for someone to pick them up bodily and transport them there. These are the people who complain that they are handicapped by circumstances. They don't have the proper working conditions: the right tools, the time, the money, the breaks.

Oh, it is a wonderful thing to have tools and money and friends and endless opportunities. But among the achieving people in all fields few have been fortunate enough to have them. Real achievement always depends upon using what you have in the best possible way while waiting for something better. As someone once put it, "Wait for a break and you'll be broke."

Nineteenth-century Czech composer Anton Dvořak might have complained that he couldn't write music because he had no money to buy printed notation paper. But the poverty-stricken youth wasted no energy in grumbling. He salvaged paper bags from the gutters of Paris, and with the stump of a pencil scribbled immortal harmonies on them. Henry Ford built his first automobile in a backyard shed. Johann Strauss wrote his exquisite "Acceleration Waltzes" on the back of a menu card while sitting in a crowded Vienna restaurant. Whistler's *Mother*, one of the most famous of all American works of art, was painted upon a secondhand canvas in a drafty, poorly lighted studio.

The blunt truth is that ideal working conditions are seldom found. If you wait for a bigger opportunity or a better opening to begin doing your best, you will probably never start. The place to make a beginning is here; the time to start is now.

A certain druggist was confident that he could make a success if only something would break for him. So he neglected his business while he looked for the better opening that never materialized. Then one day he said to himself, "Why should I try to make a start in some field I know nothing about? Why not make my own drugstore the opportunity I've been seeking?" The result was that Charles R. Walgreen built a neighborhood drugstore into a nationwide chain.

Thus it has always been. The people who get things done in the world do not sit grumbling about lack of opportunity. An Eastern legend tells of two youths who sat weaving at their looms. Each was brought a supply of yarn every morning. One day there was a large heap of the black thread of Sorrow. Dmitri rebelliously added this in harsh patches, but Ivan wove his with sympathy. Golden threads of Happiness were so few that Dmitri did not bother to pick them up; but Ivan skillfully blended them into the pattern. When eventually the Master came to inspect the tapestries, Dmitri growled, "Mine is no good because you did not give me the proper yarn." But the Master discovered Ivan's work to be a masterpiece of weaver's art, light mingling gracefully with shadow. "Each of you received the same materials," the Master said gently, "and you have used them as you wished. It is not what comes into your life that determines the pattern; it is the use you make of it."

42. The Lifters and the Leaners

Someone has said that there are only two types of persons in the world: the lifters and the leaners. It is interesting to observe both types to try to discover what makes them what they are. It doesn't seem to make much difference in what circumstances life has placed the lifters—among the wealthy or among those of moderate means—they have one characteristic in common. They manipulate life; they *use* life instead of letting life and the adverse conditions of life use them. More than this, by their example and their active effort, they are forever lifting the spirits and the loads of those around them.

On the other hand there are the leaners, those who never seem to take hold of life for themselves. The man next door whom you dread to see coming because you know he is going to talk about his steady stream of troubles—troubles that often are nothing more than the usual ones that life presents to most of us and that he magnifies out of all proportion to their importance. He is the man who always needs help, who is always being pushed, who is always at the end of his rope.

About one hundred and forty years ago, there lived in America a most unusual man by the name of John Humphrey Noyes. He was the leader of a group of persons who called themselves "perfectionists." He had many strange and unconventional ideas, but some of them were very fine. One of his sayings was: "There is too much horizontal fellowship. There should be ascending fellowship and descending fellowship." What did he mean by that? Simply that we are too prone to seek only those persons whose interests and development are similar or equal to our own. There is a need for us to seek also those whose needs are greater than our own, for we all know our own need for inspiration. And if we are going to be the channels of good that we are intended to be, there is a need for us to seek those persons whose interests and development are less than ours.

Scottish evangelist Henry Drummond once said: "There are some men and women in whose company we are always at our best. While with them we cannot think mean thoughts or speak ungenerous words. Their mere presence is elevation to us. All the best stops in our nature are drawn out by our contact with them, and we find a music in our soul that was never there before."

It is a wonderful thing to find and to be with such a person. But it is also important that we try to be that kind of person to someone else. One who has never had that sort of influence on someone has never truly lived. Not one of us is unimportant. For some other person at some time each of us may open a little gate to the kingdom of heaven. To someone today we are important!

The world is full of problems. The big problems we must leave to our statesmen to solve. In these cases, to a degree, we are required to be leaners. But in the individual's small orbit, each person may become part of the answer, part of the solution instead of continuing to be part of the problem. In this sense we can be lifters. If the economy is to be stabilized or if the world is to achieve peace, it will be done by lifters and not leaners.

43. The Master Plan!

What do you want to achieve, to accomplish? There is a simple method that can help you attain the success you truly desire. It is the master plan for success.

As you read the biographies of great men, you find that a master plan was usually followed by them or by someone near them. The success of Franklin D. Roosevelt must be attributed to a master plan drawn up by Louis Howe twenty years before FDR became President. Howe was so convinced of Roosevelt's potential as a great leader that he refused to become disturbed even when Roosevelt had his crippling illness. And Roosevelt kept to the timetable right on schedule.

If you can conceive what you wish to accomplish within the next few years, work out a timetable for your success, and then hold to that expectation, quietly working toward it. But keep the plan to yourself. Don't try to get somebody else's approval of it. The doubts of others can dissipate your dream. Your master plan will become a magnetic influence, drawing to you whatever else is needed to make your life as you wish it—if you keep it alive in your mind.

Adolf Hitler used the master plan idea destructively. He was unknown in the early 1920s—he had no money, no friends, no influence. But he created a master plan while in jail. It was outlined in his book *Mein Kampf*. It has been said that World War II might have been avoided if the world had taken Hitler's master plan seriously.

One of the great men of modern times was Winston Churchill. He was a master planner. Early in his career he wanted to get into public life but he was unknown to the public. He succeeded in getting some English papers to allow him to write for them. His vivid newspaper accounts attracted a large following and he became known to the British people. Then he began to run for various political offices. Every time he was defeated for an office, he would run for a more important one. After one defeat Churchill turned to the winner and said, "I don't think the world has heard the last of either of us." He believed in his master plan, and we saw the results in the tremendous success of his life.

Create a master plan for yourself. Fix it in your mind, and keep thinking about it secretly. Then when the way begins to open for you to achieve results, you can do so very quickly. The longer your dream is in coming, the greater it will be when it arrives.

Never underestimate the power of the master plan. It is scientific, it is practical, it is businesslike, and it works. And one important point to remember is that success has a way of coming in a hurry after you have endured a "long haul" of plodding along slowly. Have your plans made as to what you will do when success arrives. More people fail at this point than any other. They dream of success and opportunity, but the chance comes, and finds them unprepared.

Hold to your master plan in your secret heart, and keep working and keep on keeping on—and just when it may seem least likely, the tide will turn for you. You will go on to success with blessings beyond anything you could have envisioned for yourself.

44.   A Cosmic View of Work

If all you are getting out of your work is a paycheck, then you are underpaid, even if your salary runs to six figures. One of the objectives of this book is to help you to get a new positive attitude about your work, which will, in turn, give you a whole new attitude toward life.

In a time when much stress is placed on the "right to work," it may appear to be a little outdated to suggest that we need to give some thought to the "responsibilities of work." The right to work usually implies the "right to a paycheck." And, unfortunately, many people stop looking for work as soon as they get a job. People are creative beings, and the right to work is the potential for creative expression. However, there is a matter of the will that is called for to put that creative expression to good use: to give, to serve, to produce.

Ask yourself the probing question, "Why do I work?" If you answer, "Why, to make a living," then you may well be missing the real meaning of work. "Why do you breathe?" Because it is a necessity to live. And you work because you have to, because you must release your creative energy, you must express and give. You do not work to make a living, but to make a life! The living comes too. But what is a living without a life? Or as the great Teacher put it, "What doth it profit a man to gain the whole world and lose his own soul?"

How many people live out their lives in work that is drudgery to them, plodding along meaninglessly back and forth to a job that they would define as "just a living." They may not be able to change their jobs, but they can change attitudes toward their jobs. They can begin to see work in a new light, see it as an integral part of something important that the employer is trying to do. This change of attitude will change their entire experience of life, for life *is* consciousness. A street sweeper began to think of his work as "protecting the health of the community," and his life took on new meaning. Even his work became interesting.

Emerson says, "No matter what your work, let it be yours. . . . Let what you are doing be organic, let it be in your bones, and you open the door by which the affluence of heaven and earth shall stream into you." Your work is actually a cosmic activity, something you do in the process of fulfilling your inner nature. Do it in this attitude and your desk or factory bench becomes a veritable altar and every separate task becomes a wayside shrine. The exciting thing is that when you work in this spirit, the "affluence of heaven and earth streams into you," which means that you receive the material rewards too.

You may complain that your work is inferior, that it is beneath you, that it is not conducive to growth and increase. Then it is just the right place at this point in your life to do the growing you need to take the next step forward. Work always provides you with unlimited opportunities for smoothing off the rough edges of your growing character. If your work seems dull, uninteresting, or even repulsive to you, then there is something in you that needs just what this work can give. You are in your right place. If you work in nonresistance and love, you will find that either the job will change or you will be changed or moved to another one.

Ultimately work must become a joy. This is a good test: If you are not happy in your work, don't try to find what is wrong with the work, but what is wrong with the way you are doing your work. As Kalil Gibran says, "If you can't work with joy, you should leave your work and go and sit at the gate of the Temple and beg alms from those who can."

Remember, your work is your opportunity to grow as a person. When you begin your day, go forward in joy and expectation of the cosmic process that is involved in you. Determine you will work with joy and enthusiasm. Endow your work with all that you want it to be and it will be the means for demonstrating great fulfillment in your life, and affluence of living too.

45. The Healing of the Economy

Everyone talks about the faltering economy, but no one seems able to do much about it. Perhaps it is because we have thought of it as an external thing that happens *to* us, rather than a manifestation of mental states that happen *in* us. The time is at hand for leaders in all fields to realize the connection between consciousness and economics. The fluctuation of thought has as much influence on the arteries of commerce as psychosomatic medicine purports to have on the organs and functions of the body.

The difficulty in our modern society is that, with a standard of living that would boggle the mind of people of earlier times, we have lost sight of any standard *for* living. The American economy has long been a pace-setter for the world. We have generously exported money, technology, and gadgetry out of the expanse of our American dream. But in recent years, through the progressive emphasis on materialism, our exports have been going at the *expense* of our dream.

There are two great attitudes found in the pioneers who built this nation—the same attitudes that are at the root of all that has been accomplished through the years: faith, and the will to work. Wherever you look, you can see the fruits of faith: dams, bridges, skyscrapers, and aerospace technology. Regardless of business indicators, the need today is for continued faith in the infinite flow of God Mind and the limitlessness of substance. There is no lack—never has been, never can be. Substance! We may frustrate its flow; we may act from fear and block the current; but we always live and move and have being in a prodigal universe.

But we must also remember that "faith without works is dead." And there is much work to be done. The strength of this nation has always been its ingenuity, creativity, and productivity. Our Achilles heel has been our emphasis on materiality. The principle is, and our history dramatically bears this out, that when we focus on giving, doing, building, we become channels for the dynamic flow of substance, and things go well with us. When we focus on getting, on things, and rewards, mammon becomes the predominate force—and we frustrate the Divine Flow.

I believe that the major cause of our crippling inflation, unacceptable rate of unemployment, and general recession of business is in the steady erosion of the will to work. It could be said that we are at the very bottom of a great depression of worker attitudes. There has been a steady trend through industry and its workers toward greater profits for inferior products, higher wages for fewer hours, and less and less productivity. The increasingly prevalent attitude is "What's in it for me?" As long as this trend continues, the economic confusion will continue to an inevitable collapse—inevitable, that is, unless a basic change takes place.

If there could be an orchestrated resurgence of faith in the inherent affluence of the universe, and a dynamic turnaround in worker attitudes and productivity (with workers working as if the work were being done for their own homes and families), coupled with a rededication of people and the nation as a whole to transcendent goals—a contagion of believing in God instead of mammon, an epidemic of mutuality, of giving with less thought of return—the upward spiral of inflation and the sluggish performance of the economy would be reversed in a matter of weeks, and a new consciousness would rule the economy. You may feel that you are only one. But if you change your consciousness and redirect your faith and your work attitudes, things will change for you. You will become a part of the solution, rather than remaining a part of the problem of the nation's economy. You make the difference!

46. How to Find Employment

If you are unemployed or know someone who is, here is a challenging thought: There are a lot of threadbare secondhand thoughts passing for advice today. For example: "They say that times are hard. They say that there are no jobs to be had. They say that at your age there is little hope of employment." Who is this *they* who say so much? No matter what *they* say, what do *you* say? Think for yourself.

Don't let the world about you decide the climate of the world within you. Don't wait until you read the morning paper to determine how you feel. Make up your mind first that it is a good day. Refuse to shape your thoughts by the market returns. These simply reflect the fluctuations of the nation's confidence. Think for yourself. Did you know that it is possible to think positively about employment and actually find a job even in time of mass unemployment? It is also possible to think fearfully about your job even in times of prosperity, and be laid off from your seemingly secure job. "That which I feared hath come upon me," said Job.

Another question—and it's a blunt one—Are you looking for work, or are you just looking for a job? Are you trying to get on a payroll somewhere, or are you really interested in becoming a hard-working creative asset to some company? Is work something you enjoy doing, or is it simply, as the man says,

"You've gotta eat"? No organization will long retain a person, if they hire him at all, whose attitudes and interests are that vague and unrelated to the goals of the company.

When you find a job, or are called back to one you had— or—even if you simply start out in the morning to a job you now have—do you say, "Well, back to the salt mines! Back to the old drag!" This kind of thinking must go! Never go back to work. Always go forward to work. *Back to work* is something you *have* to do. *Forward to work* is more than likely what you *want* to do. How often it is said, "Many people stop looking for work as soon as they have found a job." This is one of the real problems of our time. Don't let it be your problem!

No one wants just another name on the payroll, but there is many an employer who is desperately in need of someone to help with the work. If you believe you can help and can convey that sincere belief, you will find work.

Regarding the matter of age, Richard D. Gleason, a job consultant who has guided the careers of hundreds of executives, says that it is not true that few employers will hire men or women over forty. He says that age is rarely the *reason* but almost always the *excuse* an employer gives for not hiring. The real reason, he says, is that the applicant has not shown the spirit of giving, has not emphasized what he can do for the employer.

If you are looking for work, therefore, get your mind filled with the true spirit of service, and it may well be that the "world will beat a path to your door."

47. Giving Yourself Away

I once heard a story about a good man who went to a neighborhood parish to preach by invitation and took his young son with him. When he entered the church he saw a contribution box conspicuously placed, and in obedience to his good instincts, he deposited a half a dollar. After he had made his address and was departing, his preacher-host said to him: "We are not a very prosperous parish, and all that we can pay you is what is in the contribution box." He then opened the box and presented to his visitor the half dollar—all that had been put in. The visitor thanked him and went his way, if not rejoicing, at least resigned.

Pretty soon his little boy, who had been a witness to the proceedings, looked up and said: "Pop, if you had put more in, you would have gotten more out."

Wisdom from the mouth of babes! This is really the law of life: we get back only as much as we put in. It is a universal principle that is operative constantly for saint and sinner alike, for rich and poor, for young and old, for Easterner and Westerner—whether we know it or not, whether we like it or not.

One of the great delusions of our time is that you can get something for nothing. All the religions of the ages have taught that we reap as we sow, that we receive in life what we earn.

Ralph Waldo Emerson wrote an essay entitled "Compensation" that should be required reading for every young person about to start out in the world of commerce. In it he says,

In labor as in life there can be no cheating. The thief steals from himself. The swindler swindles himself.... A wise man will ... pay every just demand on [his] time, [his] talents, [his] heart. Always pay; for first or last you must pay your entire debt.... The benefit we receive must be rendered again, line for line, deed for deed, cent for cent, to somebody.

We would save ourselves an awful lot of trouble in life if we learned this lesson early.

It seems to me that the key to the whole matter is in our basic attitude toward life. Is life a matter of what we can get out of it, or what we can put into it? If we can once and for all realize that *you can't get something for nothing*, that we receive only as we give, then we will begin to think of life in terms of giving.

There was a fine book a few years ago based on this great truth. Its title: *Try Giving Yourself Away*. I say, no matter what your occupation or business or profession, your true business is the *express business*, the business of expressing your divinely endowed talents and attributes. Yes, "try giving yourself away!" You may be surprised.

Sometime in the next few days in practically every commercial office or plant in America an important executive will sit back and study a list of names on a sheet of paper. Your name could well be on it. A position of responsibility is open and the executive is face to face with the old, old problem: "Where can I find the right person?" The faces, the words, the work, the impressions of various men and women will pass through his mind in quick review. Whom will he select? Well, what do you think?

He will select the applicant who has evidenced the greatest spirit of service, who has shown the greatest interest in working rather than in getting paid for work, who has not shunned responsibility. The applicant who has been thinking "give" instead of "receive."

It may be difficult for you to believe that *you can't get something for nothing*, especially when it would appear that many do, but I say, just act as if you did believe, let the theme of your life be "giving" instead of "getting," and you will not only find the one sure way to success, but you will be happy in the bargain.

48. From Futility to Significance

One of the great problems of this age is the frustration of living without a purpose. J. P. Marquand in his play "Point of no Return" has one of the principal characters observe of another, "He knew all the little answers, but he missed the large questions." We know how to get ahead in business, how to keep life well-dressed and upholstered, how to have a shiny new car and the tallest television aerial, but what of the big questions? What is life all about?

In our day, despite the fact that we are surrounded with one of the highest living standards in world history, with conveniences and comforts beyond the wildest dreams of our forebears, we are often classed as a nation of disturbed people. Our high incidence of mental illness is undeniable, a fact often explained as the result of the pace of our mechanical age and the speed of living that seems to be inseparable from an urban society in our day. And yet a survey into the incidence of mental illness has shown that it is particularly high in the state of Kansas, which is one of our least urban areas, while on the other hand there are men and women in the bustling cities of New York and Chicago who are in no danger of getting the disease at all.

One of the real root causes of mental illness and all the related emotional disturbances may one day be identified as a sense of the meaninglessness and futility of life. There is a suggestion of this in Paul Osborn's play *Morning's at Seven*, in which Carl, a white-haired dentist, periodically suffers from what the family politely called "spells." When these "spells" come on he goes about frantically asking everyone, "Where am I?" This does not refer to geographical location. What troubles him is, "Where am I after sixty years of living? Though I have made a good living, have I made a good life? Have I fully used my possibilities?"

Every once in a while I have an opportunity to watch a group of successful businesspeople celebrating something or other. Many of them will be more than moderately intoxicated. Often I ask myself, Why? Why do these people, some of them out-standingly successful, make fools of themselves? They would be incredulous if they were told they were running away from a meaningless existence. They are actually having a "spell," like Carl, and asking themselves, "Where am I?" Sadly enough, they have no answer.

Scientific studies of the use of alcohol, notably those carried on at Yale University, show conclusively that alcoholism is the result of spiritual lack or emptiness, or living without a purpose. Someone for whom life has lost its meaning turns to alcohol as a substitute. Thus alcoholism can be cured only by a new sense of significance, rather than by trying to correct symptoms.

Somehow we get off the track in life, getting all wrapped up in ourselves as if we were the proprietors and not the trustees of the gifts of God. We think of life as a grim business of competition and acquisition. But we have it all wrong. The purpose is not to make a living, but to make a life—not to amass but to express. Step out of selfish thinking and living into selfless giving and serving, and you take a giant step from futility to significance.

49. The Feel of Success

There is an old saying, "There's nothing that succeeds like success." Why? Because there is no way you can succeed in any venture unless you have the *feeling of success*. And when you have the success feeling, the mind is set for success, and there is no way that you can fail.

You know the person who works hard, who is sincere, who does all the things that should produce results, but who fails every time. "Poor John," we say, "nothing ever works right for him!" But John is poor because John is a loser. I don't mean he is unlucky or that he was *born* to lose; John is a loser because he has a self-image of inadequacy. He thinks failure. He is his own obstacle to success. But it doesn't have to be that way. John can change. He too can be successful, if he can just achieve that mental feeling of success. But unless he makes that inward change, he will continue to fail, to feel sorry for himself, and to be held up as the perfect example of the injustice of life.

What is it you want to do or be? Can you think of this goal in terms of a present possibility? If you can't, perhaps you are working in the wrong direction. How would you feel if the thing you are working for were now accomplished? Think about it! You would feel thrilled and happy, fulfilled and satisfied. You may say that it is hard to get a feeling of a thing before it is accomplished. But actually, you do it all the time. When you are worried about something that is to happen in the future, you experience all the same emotions in advance that would overwhelm you if the thing feared *were* to happen. Worry about failure often leads to negative experiences.

There is a creative power in the mind that constantly works to produce in our experience that which is most strongly felt. Get the positive goal in mind, picture it to yourself so vividly as to make it "real," and think of it in terms of the accomplished fact—and you will be armed with the success feeling. The result: You will be buoyed up with self-confidence, courage, and a flow of creative ideas. When the mind is "set" for success, the positive result will seem to move toward you as relentlessly as you may be working toward its achievement.

Avoid, as a plague, the tendency, in discouragement, to recall past failures. Instead recall successes, even in simple things like winning a game of tennis. Recall how you felt in winning, in succeeding. When you reactivate the success patterns out of the past, you will restore the success feeling that accompanied them. If you can recapture that success feeling, you will evoke all the winning actions that produced the successful results.

J. C. Penney, founder of the vast merchandising chain, tells how he heard his father say on his deathbed, "I know Jim will make it." And from that time onward, Penney felt that he would succeed—somehow—although he had no tangible assets, no money, no education. Whenever he became discouraged, he would remember this prediction of his father's, and he would "feel" that somehow he would make it, and make it he did! Another man who had a history of failure told a counselor of overhearing an uncle say, "Steve will never amount to anything; no one in this family ever has." This subconscious feeling had blocked his path. So he replaced it with a goal and with the image of its accomplishment, and the chronic failure became a winner.

Remember, success begins with success—it begins in the mind. Get the success habit by making a habit of picturing the successful achievement of everything you undertake. You can be a winner if you get the winning feeling. Right now, say to yourself: "I am a success!" Not, "I hope to be," "someday I will be," or even, "please God let me be"—but "I am a success!"

50. Do You Have Soft Shoulders?

Some years ago an item appeared in a St. Louis, Missouri, newspaper. It said that the public library on one day had recovered seventeen hundred books, including one overdue thirty-three years. Fines on overdue books were suspended that day, "Forgiveness Day." The moment the library extended this invitation, conscience-free borrowers, relieved of all responsibility and obligation, hastened to return the "borrowed property."

You might be thinking, "How can people be so dishonest!" But you know, this is not dishonesty at all—as was proven by the fact that the books were quickly returned when it was made easy. It is simply an evidence of an all-too-common lack of responsibility. One person may say, "So what, everyone is doing it. Who will ever know, anyway?" A worker may say, "Why should I knock myself out in my work? What will it get me? You have to have seniority to get a promotion anyway. So I say, do as little as you can get by with, keep out of sight, and show up on payday."

There is a single reason why ninety-nine out of one hundred average businessmen never become leaders. They have soft shoulders. They are unwilling to assume responsibility. When a job is given them they unburden it on the first person who will accept it. The world, however, is stabilized by those who take responsibilities. Someone has to do everything that is done. The greatest satisfaction in life comes in fulfilling responsibility and not dodging duty; in meeting and solving problems; in facing facts; and becoming a dependable person.

It is quite likely that the reason we tend to shy away from responsibility is the subtle fear that we will be overburdened. Now, there is little question but that added responsibilities mean added work. As one executive recently quipped, "Work faithfully for eight hours a day and don't worry; then in time you may become the boss and work sixteen hours a day and have all the worries."

Of course, that is not the whole story. There is a saying that if you want a job done, give it to the busy man to do. The busy man has geared himself to using his time and talents wisely. I strongly suspect that he has become successful because of the development that added responsibilities brought about.

This is the inference to be drawn from a ten-year study of people in various occupations conducted by the General Motors Research Institute. This study showed that as workers advanced to positions of increasing responsibility, their mental and emotional stability increased markedly, as did their ability to withstand strain. On the other hand, psychological tests showed that those who did not rise appreciably in occupational status during the ten-year period showed no improvement in personality adjustment whatever.

Josiah Gilbert Holland, American editor and writer, once said: "Responsibility walks hand in hand with capacity and power." In other words responsibility is actually an opportunity and a stimulant to growth. We never really come to know the possibilities of our nature until we are challenged in some way. Perhaps the key to the word "responsibility" is in our response. The ability must be within us inherently or, in the cosmic law of life, the challenge would not have come. But how do we react to it?

Emerson writes of this:

> So nigh is grandeur to our dust,
>   So near is God to man,
> When duty whispers low, Thou must,
>   The Youth replies, I can.

51. Your Work as a "Calling"

We have long accepted the idea that ministers and priests and rabbis are *called* to do God's work, but actually every kind of work is a calling as far as the individual who performs it is concerned. The word "vocation" comes from the root word "voco" (I call). Can you think of your job as a sacred calling?

We miss the whole idea of work if we consider it only in the framework of theological idealism. On the other side of the coin, we are distracted from the true purpose of work when we measure it by the amount of money it pays and the amount of time it takes to pay it. The "calling" to a vocation taps one's inherent talent or inclination. It is important that early in life we learn to read the handwriting on the wall of our creative personalities so that we will not become the square peg in the round hole, or vice versa.

There are many available resources for determining our calling, for example, aptitude tests or employment counselors. But none of these does much good until we resolve one problem in our thinking. Is the purpose of life to make a living, or to live your making? The former attitude leads innumerable people to financial success accompanied by creative frustration. The latter attitude keeps one in a perpetual state of searching within and without for the clues to the purpose in one's life.

It seems to me that people are endowed with a certain genius for the kind of work they are chosen to do. This doesn't mean that everyone can be a great artist or a skillful scientist. But it does mean that everyone can be creative and happy in a service that is important to mankind, whether it be sweeping the heavens in an observatory or in sweeping the streets of Manhattan. Of course, I do not mean to imply that you can step into your chosen work without training and preparation. I simply mean that, important as training is, it is not the only needed preparation. Unless one has felt the "call," one lives only to work and any amount of technical training is likely to prove inadequate to achieve unusual excellence.

I often think of two teachers in the same school. One had just enough training to qualify for his position, with little skill in mathematics, but he had been blessed with genius as a teacher. The other had advanced graduate degrees in mathematics, but his genius was for research rather than teaching. When the highly trained teacher was out of town, the man to whom the subject was not a major interest conducted the class. During this time in the class the difficult formulas were presented in a simple and understandable way, showing the importance of having a teacher who was called to his work. Fortunately the highly trained mathematician was invited to take charge of an important institution for research. There he promptly proceeded to make himself famous. Each of these men became eminent in the field to which he was called. Neither would have been so in the other's place. That is how important it is to know that all work is a "calling" rather than just a job.

You owe it to yourself, and to those whose lives are influenced so very much by whether or not you are happy or satisfied or successful, to find your own calling. You must seek to find the insight to see your present work as a calling. It will give you the satisfaction of excellence, and it will give the world the benefit of the services of genius. Now, you may little dream that you are a genius. But you do have a particular genius for doing something in a unique and excellent manner. What do you really enjoy doing? Often you find the keys to your calling in your hobbies and outside interests. Follow your genius and you will soon be doing work that is both fulfilling and remunerative.

VI. Standing Up to Life

52. How to Make Decisions

If you have been plagued with indecision, or if you have a decision to make right now that is resting heavy on your heart, here are some thoughts that you might find helpful.

The prophet Joel once cried out, "Multitudes, multitudes, in the valley of decision!" Fortunes have been lost, opportunities passed up, chances for happiness gone glimmering, and minds left seething with unrest because many individuals have not schooled themselves in the fine art of making up their minds.

Life demands that you make decisions about many things every day. Some are of little consequence, but others can affect the course of your life. Indecision comes from fear. We are afraid to make the wrong move, to do the wrong thing, say the wrong word. Often we simply procrastinate—put off making a decision and thus put off action until that "tomorrow" that never comes.

You can learn to make decisions easily. You have hunches or flashes of insight. This is simply the activity of cosmic intelligence in you which always knows, filtering through your own blocked mind. You may have been too involved in human thought, too worried, too tense to perceive it. It is quite possible to have "hunches-to-order" when we accept their validity and make our minds receptive to their guidance.

There are two chief problems that keep us from accepting and following the inner guidance of intuition: (1) We do not have clearly defined goals. Too often we live like a child in a toy store: grabbing one thing, only to throw it aside as soon as we glimpse something else which we think we might like better. Right or wrong, set a course, have a plan; (2) We have a bad habit of not carrying through to completion action that has been determined upon. When you start something, always see it through to completion. Be a bold starter and a determined finisher.

Here is a technique for making decisions easily, confidently, and wisely. I have found it amazingly helpful. These five important steps will work for you:

First, declare for yourself, "I am fully capable of making a right decision in this matter." Nothing is accomplished without faith and confidence. No matter how many wrong decisions you think you have made in the past, you have made some right ones too. Hold on to these, for they tell you that you can make a right decision.

Second, and this is a subtle point, declare for yourself, "I cannot, I will not, make a wrong decision." You may look back on many times when an unwise choice led to problems, but the fact that you can see today that the choice *was* unwise indicates that you have done some growing. The mistake, if such it was, led to learning. The Duke of Wellington once said, "There is no mistake, there has been no mistake, there shall be no mistake." This leads to the confidence and fearlessness that is vital to decisiveness.

Third, get still. Take time to quietly reflect on the whole matter, releasing the superconscious forces of your mind. Call this prayer, call it meditation, call it quiet reasoning—it doesn't matter—but do it. The intuitive forces of your mind, far more resourceful than you realize, will go to work for you.

Fourth, keep still! Don't go around asking advice from everyone you meet. You probably have a deadline by which time the decision must be made. If not, give yourself a deadline. Now, you are ready to give the problem to your mind, and have a mental incubation period during which you can forget it. And above all, don't dissipate yourself in talking. Keep your tongue between your teeth, and your vocal chords still.

Finally, when the appointed time arrives, act, take a step, choose a course of action, do something! Even if the inspiration is not with you, open your mouth and speak. You will find yourself speaking words, taking action that seems almost foreign to you. The intuitive faculty of your mind will come into play, you will choose wisely, and you will feel secure in your choice.

To review the technique:

1. Affirm that you *can* make a right decision.

2. Declare that you cannot and will not make a wrong decision.

3. Get still in quiet meditation to release the superconscious force.

4. Keep still, don't talk, don't worry.

5. And then *act*; open your mouth and speak, and out will come the right and wise decision.

It may sound simple, but it will work for you. Try it!

53. Up-to-Par Insurance

"Thou madest him to have dominion over the works of thy hands; thou hast put all things under his feet" (Ps. 8:6, KJV). This means you! You were created to be the master of fate and circumstance. Your thoughts do not have to be reactive. You can think the kind of thoughts that you want to see unfolding in your life. You have the capacity to be "up to par"—and not just occasionally, as something to cheer about, but all the time.

A great fallacy of human thinking is that such things as joy and love and zest for life are simply the effects of good experiences. This is in error. Enthusiastic people are not that way because things are going well with them; rather, things are going well because they are enthusiastic. Happy people do not need something to be happy about; they *are* happy. And happy people seem always to attract the kind of experiences and relationships that justify happiness.

The expression "up to par" originated in England many years ago. A man named Thomas Parr, who lived to the age of 152, became such a legend that "feeling up to par" was adopted as an expression of feeling dynamically alive, a kind of "keeping up with Thomas Parr." Parr must have had a great desire to live. Charles Fillmore said that no one ever dies until he gives up. If there is a desire for life, the health process will find some way to unfold no matter what the age or the medical diagnosis.

American poet and author Stephen Vincent Benét once said, "Life is not lost by dying. Life is lost minute by minute, day by bedragging day, in all the thousand small uncaring ways." You do not lose enthusiasm because you are getting old; you begin to age through the loss of enthusiasm. You can be the victim of advancing years or you can be their master. Dr. Eric Berne says that supremely enlightened people use just three words in life:

"Yes," "no," and "wow!" (the latter, to express a healthy childlike wonder).

The question is: Are you willing to take responsibility for your life? We often delude ourselves that our problems are caused by the world "out there." We think we are "down" because of what "he" did or what "they" are saying. Things will be different we say. Things will change. Actually, the way we feel has little to do with things or persons and everything to do with how we react to them. To get "up" again, we need only to change our thoughts.

Most of the things we get "down" about are like little pebbles. Hold a pebble close to your eyes and it fills your whole world. Hold it at a proper viewing distance and it can be examined and properly dealt with. Drop the pebble at your feet and it becomes part of the gravel of the path you walk on. ("I have set all things under your feet.")

You can be "up to par" all the time if you have the desire to be, and if you are willing to "stir up the gift of God that is within you." Someone once said, "Every person contains within himself the wherewithal to surpass himself." Wherever you are, whatever your problems, and however deep you may be in the morass of depression, you can "come to yourself," you can rise phoenix-like from the ashes of defeat and self-limitation, and you can recover your equilibrium.

In a very real sense your whole day is conditioned in two five-minute periods: on awakening in the morning, and just before sleep at night. To ensure that we keep up to par in the face of life's exigencies, we need to establish some creative habits of spiritual discipline for these periods.

Prepare yourself for the day by resolving first thing on awakening that you will face the day with the highest perspective. Take a few minutes for deep breathing, holding the thought that as your lungs are being filled expansively, your whole being is being filled with the "inspiration of the Almighty."

A good drill for relaxation and sleep at night: Think of a compass needle that points north unless it is attracted by some metallic object. Remove that object and the needle returns inexorably to north. This suggests a great thought: you do not have to strain to get close to God. Just let go of anxieties and there is an immediate return to oneness.

You can keep yourself up to par, for there is that in you that is always in the Divine Flow. Pause often to remember that God has given you dominion. Keep yourself in the thought of oneness in the Divine Flow, and you will be sustained in a mental, emotional, and physical condition of "par." You may not live to be 152, as Thomas Parr did, but you will live deeply and fully and abundantly.

54. Your Innate Power to Overcome

One of the greatest achievements of this life is to have a real power over your difficulties. The reaction of the individual to difficulty marks the kind of person he or she is. It was Washington Irving, I believe, who said, "Little minds are tamed and subdued by misfortune. Great minds rise above it."

I remember reading a magazine article by Clinton P. Anderson, who was at that time a senator from New Mexico. In it he told of the lowest moment of his life. He was twenty-one years of age and had just launched out on what looked to be a promising career in the newspaper business in his home town in North Dakota. He was eagerly anticipating getting married. Then all his hopes for the future were shattered when it was discovered that he had tuberculosis.

He was sent to New Mexico where he was confined to bed in a sanitorium. There he had nothing to look forward to but death. The doctor even wired his father to come within five days if he wanted to see his son alive. His first night in the sanitorium was made even darker by a boy in the next room who cried all night for his mother, then died at daybreak. Senator Anderson said that he looked at the bottle of poisonous rubbing alcohol on the table by his bed and vaguely considered it to end his misery.

Then he realized that someone was standing beside his bed. It was an old tubercular by the name of Joe Maas. The words Joe Maas spoke to young Anderson literally saved his life. "Remember this," the older man said, in the husky whisper of the advanced tuberculosis case, "what you got will never kill you, if you keep it in your chest. But if you let it get up here," and he tapped his temple significantly, "it's fatal. Worrying kills more patients than tuberculosis itself ever did."

The veteran's words made young Anderson's heart leap, and he determined to keep thoughts of illness out of his mind. He sent for his typewriter and had it suspended from the ceiling on a pulley. Each morning, propped on a pillow, he lowered the machine onto his lap and went to work writing sketches, poems, and short stories. As he improved, he began working on the hospital newspaper, writing short features about new patients. To the patients he passed on Joe Maas's warning against letting their physical ailment become also a mental ailment. He noted in his diary the mental attitude of two thousand patients he interviewed. In nearly every instance those with a cheerful, hopeful outlook survived.

Senator Anderson himself not only had a complete recovery, but developed in that period of his life a strength of character and of thought that led him to greatness as an individual and a leader of men. He said in this article that he was where he was because Joe Maas taught him to keep his problems where they belonged, and not to let them get into the mind. He wrote that Joe Maas's advice saved his life more than once through the years and provided him with great peace and strength.

Each of us needs at times a Joe Maas to speak such words of wisdom to us when we begin to allow some trouble—an illness, a bad financial break, a tragedy, a sorrow—to monopolize our thoughts. May I be a Joe Maas for you at this moment? Remember, good friend, no matter how final it may seem, refuse to let your trouble take over your mind and lord it over your thoughts.

55. Handle Your Fears!

Someone has said that fear is the only evil in the world. Startling as it may seem it is fear that drives men to all forms of so-called evil. It is fear that makes men sick. It is fear that drives them to dishonesty and crime. It is fear that makes people inhuman to others.

People who go off with a chip on their shoulders in the morning have usually made at least two or three others miserable before noon. The whole reason for the chip on their shoulders is their defensive attitude, which comes from fear. They are afraid inside, though they may not know what they are afraid of—it may be the fear of launching out and failing, the fear of meeting people and being disliked, or a fear of the future and of the past. It may be fear of sickness, accidents, business recession, or failure, if people are afraid inside, they pick on people outside.

Fearful people hear insults where none are intended, fancy slights where none were meant, suspect others of cheating, or of plotting against them or of talking unkindly or even maliciously about them. Uncontrolled, this attitude goes on, multiplying itself until it populates the world with evil people with evil designs, and with bogeymen behind every bush. A mind so beset becomes cynical and cannot see the goodness that is inherent in all people.

Joshua Liebman in his book *Peace of Mind* says that fears are "part of the fee we pay for citizenship in an unpredictable universe." But he goes on to say, "If it is normal for us to experience fear and worry, it is also possible to master these enemies of serenity."

How can we master our fears? I would like to give you a magic formula, if I had one. But there *is* no such formula. For most of us it means simply mastering our emotions, and keeping control of our thoughts in the face of the changing and often disturbing experiences of life.

James K. Kraft, founder of the food industry that bears his name, used to tell this story on himself. He had gathered many anxieties and fears and he would take them home with him at night and disturb the family by talking about them at the dinner table. They would haunt him in the night and disturb his sleep.

One day he was inspired to develop a single technique for dealing with his anxieties that proved surprisingly beneficial. He lived in a residental suburb and had a fence around his home with a mailbox at the gate. During the day as he became aware of being fearful about anything, he would write his fears down on cards and put the cards in his pocket. He said this was helpful, because when he saw the fears and worries in black and white they seemed to leave the hazy recesses of his mind.

When he reached home in the evening he would put the cards in his mailbox, saying, "I now entrust these fears into the care of the infinite mind of the universe." Then he would go into the house and relax and play with his family and have a good night's sleep. In the morning he would take the cards from the mailbox and look them over on his way to work. He would be amazed at how many of them he could now discard, realizing the fears written on them were unnecessary ones. For those that needed more thought he would take the appropriate cards with him for further constructive work. If any were still not solved he would put them back in the mailbox that night. He says he did this for years, and that it was the one reason that he could live a happy and relaxed life, despite the heavy pressures of business.

Childish and simple you say? Yes, but practical and workable too, and that is what counts, isn't it?

You may not have a house with a mailbox at the fencepost, and you may not be impressed by this simple technique; but it is certain that most of the great fears of life can be handled by steadfastly meeting them in some similar way.

56. Stand Up to Life

Someone has called this "the age of worry." Certainly there are a lot of worried people. And it would seem that there is plenty in the world to worry about. And yet, it would seem to me that eventually we would come to realize the complete futility of worry.

Suppose that worry could be put into a bottle labeled: "Danger—this medicine is good for nothing whatsoever. It will reduce the number of red corpuscles in your blood. It will interfere with your heart. It will derange the proper functioning of your internal glands. It will poison your whole system and rob you of your vitality. It will cloud the brain and befuddle your thinking. It will eat the lining out of your stomach, and will make you miserable." Would you drink such a potion? Would you argue that you simply must drink it because you anticipated some trouble? Sounds ridiculous when we put it in this way, doesn't it?

Why then do we worry? It is likely that we worry because "it's a little habit we've acquired." Someone will say, "Now just a minute, I can't help worrying with all the problems I have. You would be worried too if you were in my place." I well might be, if I were a worrier. But you see, no one makes us worry; we impose it upon ourselves. For every person worried over a specific problem, you will find somewhere another person meeting the same sort of problem with faith and an untroubled heart. We worry precisely because we determine that is the way we are going to meet our difficulty. Once you learn that you can just refuse to "push the worry button," you take a great step forward into happy and effective living.

There is a delightful story told of Rossini, the famous nineteenth-century Italian composer. It seems that the first night that his opera *The Barber of Seville* was produced, it was very badly received. Hisses and cries of derision followed the fall of the curtain. The prima donna was in hysterics. The leading man talked darkly of suicide. Then they looked for the composer, but Rossini was nowhere to be found.

"The worst has happened," cried the distraught manager, "the *maestro* has destroyed himself." They rushed off in a body to Rossini's lodgings and discovered him—sound asleep in bed. They woke him up, crying, "*Maestro*, are you all right?" Rossini replied, "I was having a nice sleep before you woke me up." They said, "But the opera, fiasco!" Rossini replied, "Evidently *The Barber* is not good enough; so I must compose something better, that is all; but we will discuss that in the morning. Now please let me sleep." And he relapsed into slumber.

Of course we know that *The Barber of Seville* turned out to be an immense success, playing steadily for over a hundred years. The story demonstrates that the habit of keeping peaceful and poised, of standing up to life, is the key to a life free from worry.

It seems to me that there are always many different levels upon which we may appraise any situation. Worry comes from an unusually persistent analysis of things from the lowest possible point of view. If we stand up to our problems, we stand tall as individuals and we tend to see things from a higher perspective. Ralph Waldo Emerson once said, "Prayer is the contemplation of the facts of life from the highest point of view." Whether we call it prayer or leaning upon the intuitive forces of our mind or simply positive and constructive thinking—when we stand up to life and refuse to push the worry button, we are on the road to anxiety-free living.

57. People Who Live in the Wilderness

History is a good teacher, but in one respect it is inadequate. It records the story of Henry Ford, for example, whose venturesome spirit led to a whole new way of life in America. But where do we find the names of Ford's contemporaries, whose mechanical skill might have been comparable to Ford's, but who did not venture forth?

From history we can learn what to avoid from its bad examples, and from her finest men we can learn what goals to seek, but we are not warned of the dangers of inactivity, because history does not record the story of those who never tried. Yet this is one of man's greatest perils! If thousands fail from lack of judgment or from limited ability, millions fail because they never even try.

Fortunately we do have at least one dramatic record in the Old Testament of ten men who were afraid to venture forward, and who infected a whole nation with their hesitancy. According to the ancient story in Numbers, the Israelites, on reaching the border of The Promised Land, sent a squad of twelve men to seek out the prospects. The twelve returned with glowing records of the possibilities of the country, but only two of them felt their nation was able to accept the challenge. The other ten mourned that there were giants in the land, adding dolefully, "and we were in our sight as grasshoppers, and so we were in their sight."

Well, the nation followed the counsel of the ten, and the Israelites wandered in the wilderness for forty years, until a new generation, with courage and faith to act, rose up and entered the Land of Promise.

People who live in the wilderness! Every community is full of them. They admit they could get more out of life, perhaps they even declare that they expect someday to enter their own promised land; but they idle away their years complaining about the size of the obstacles in their path. This stay-where-you-are, take-no-chances attitude is demonstrated in every phase of life.

There is a law that is written all through life: *If we do not go forward, we slip backward.* We cannot long stand in the same spot.

Now, of course, we should not be rash. Of course we should look before we leap. But the trouble with most of us is that we look too long; then, our strength ebbing, we fail to leap at all. And the man who will not venture eventually finds himself living in the wilderness of life, plodding in endless circles.

Take a good look at the land, as did the Israelites, yes. But after considering the challenge before you, remind yourself of your hidden resources. Remember that life is on your side. Growth is a fundamental law of the universe, and the man who ventures forward is moving with the law.

How very many people continue on the treadmill because they feel that they missed their chance. Biographies prove that it is never too late. In every college today men and women, middle-aged and beyond, are embarking upon the educational programs they missed in their youth. Opportunity knocks again and again for those who are willing to receive it.

Once you begin to move forward, you will be surprised at the tide that begins to flow in your direction. You will discover that the wilderness of defeat and oblivion was of your own making. Move out of the wilderness of your doubts and fears, and you will find that life is on your side.

For every one of us there is a wilderness, and for each of us there is a promised land. Each of us must decide for himself where to pitch the tent. One thing is certain—those who are willing to venture forth will not long be lost in the wilderness of defeat.

58. How to Meet Interruptions

Have you ever had one of those days when it seemed that it was impossible to get anything done because of a constant stream of interruptions? The English poet Coleridge once started a poem. He had the whole pattern clearly in mind and eagerly wrote down the first few lines. At that moment he was called to the door by a man from Porlock, and he was detained on business for an hour. When he returned the whole inspiration for the poem had left him.

I suspect that the "man from Porlock" knocks on many a door. He may be the salesman who wants to sell a set of books without which no home is complete, or he may be an illness and hospitalization, or a beating in the stock market. And he may contribute to a loss of inspiration, of time, of money, and—worst of all—of patience and peace of mind.

We may cry out, "Why can't people leave me alone? Why does everything happen to me?" But honestly, does this sort of resistance do any good? Life is change. Interruptions are simply a part of the scenery. Without the interruptions of change, could there be any growth or progress, or anything of interest in life?

Today psychologists are vitally concerned with mental health. They tell us that we need to cultivate a resiliency of spirit, so that we can bend like a tree before the wind, but not break. The manufacturers of automobile tires tried at first to make a tire that would resist the shocks of the road, but this tire was quickly torn to shreds. Then they started making tires that would give a little and absorb shocks. These tires are still with us; they endure because they are resilient.

It seems to me that we need to meet every day in the spirit of adventure, expecting interesting and profitable experiences. Then when interruptions come, we do not fight them, but rather we make the most of them and draw forth the best from them. It is in this spirit that interruptions can actually be the "spice of life." I know a man who had an unbelievable series of crises in the past few years and has every reason to be despondent. Not so. He laughingly says, "Well at least there is nothing dull about my life. And I can tell you this, I have found a lot of hidden resources that I never dreamed I possessed."

Some time ago a newspaper carried two interesting stories. One young man left this note on a bridge: "To whom it may concern; I am going to jump off this bridge because the only one I ever loved is mad at me." The other was a brief editorial comment on a young Air Force corporal who, when his girl jilted him, wrote a song that became a hit and earned him fifty thousand dollars. The paper drew this moral: when you lose your girl, don't jump off a bridge—turn your sorrow into a song.

When the "man from Porlock" knocks at your door, don't resist the interruption. He may bring good news. At least it can become good, if you determine to make it so. You may not finish the poem or the important report. But you may help a friend, or write a song, or find some new undreamed of good.

59. Taking the Simple Way

Have you ever heard someone remark about the actions of another, "What's the matter with that person? Any fool would know better than that!" It is true that there are certain ways marked out in life, marked so plainly that "wayfaring men, though fools, shall not err therein." But it is also strangely true that we are all at times a little foolish. Sometimes it seems that the easy way, the simple answer, isn't what we want.

Rube Goldberg, creator of those fabulous cartoons that illustrate the needlessly complex means we sometimes use to arrive at simple solutions, shows a man in bed surrounded and nearly obscured by a complicated device that tips his bed up—and him out of it—at a certain time in the morning. The cartoon is always terribly funny because of the obvious simplicity of the solution. How much easier it would be for the man to set the alarm clock, and then have the courage to jump out of bed when it rings!

In mathematics we are told that a straight line is the shortest distance between two points. Obviously the simple solution is to go directly to the objective. And yet it sometimes seems that we want to wander around in the wilderness; that we want prescriptions with unpronounceable names; that we want trading stamps with our purchases even though we know that we are paying more for them in the price of the items bought; that we want to give long, wordy explanations when a simple "yes" or "no" answer would suffice; that we embark upon one program after another in seeking to lose weight—crash diets and "blitz" diets, along with pills and dietary supplements—when the simple way would be to get up from the table when we are still hungry, and lock the kitchen door after hours.

Actually, the solutions to some of our problems are much more simple than is sometimes supposed—not necessarily easy (nor even particularly palatable), but simple—as simple as spending less than we earn to correct a financial problem or not talking to correct the habit of saying the wrong thing; as simple as thinking only positive and constructive things to create a happy and fulfilling life experience. Why concoct a complicated, hard-to-understand and harder-to-follow solution? Why not seek and follow the simple way?

I sometimes wonder if we were not better off in the matter of raising children before we knew about complexes and inhibitions and aggression and repression. I wonder if most of us do not become amateur psychologists and then seek out complicated diagnoses. We used to call it "two-faced," but now we say someone is displaying "schizophrenic tendencies." The result is that we can't see the forest for the trees, and what is worse, the trees are of our own planting. Without our insistence on the complex way, we could see both the problem and its solution with ease.

Perhaps there is no absolutely painless way of solving a grievous problem. There may be no truly painless way of getting out of debt or renouncing a habit such as smoking or drinking. There may be no easy, effortless way to make a lot of money, or to get ahead, or to be a star. There may be no altogether pleasant and palatable way to lose weight or to learn to speak a foreign language. But there is usually a *simple* way, if we will face the facts, get back to first principles, and remember that most problems are the creations of our own minds, and most solutions are as close to us as our inmost intuitive thoughts.

60. Your Genius for Good Fortune

It is amazing how widespread is the belief that life's fortune is determined by the flip of a coin. Many people refer to sickness or unemployment as "bad luck." Often someone says, "I have been down on my luck lately." It is interesting how we hear people impute all their misfortunes to bad luck, while their successes or good fortune they ascribe to their own cleverness.

The belief in luck or chance has been one of the most self-limiting attitudes of the whole human race. It crowds out real faith and lulls all true initiative to sleep. As Emerson once put it, "Small men believe in luck; wise men believe in cause and effect."

Life is not a game of chance. "Qué Sera, Sera" may be a good song, but "what will be, will be" is an abominable philosophy. Life's experiences are regulated by the activity of causation, which is never completely divorced from the consciousness of the individual. We are living magnets, constantly drawing to ourselves the things, people, and circumstances that are in accord with our thoughts.

The greatest mistake people can make is to insist that a twist of fate can ruin their lives. One man who was dismissed from his job recently is bordering on a complete mental collapse. He says, "My life is over. This is the end of everything." He talks of the lucky break he had in getting the job many years ago, and he wonders how this could come to him now. Actually, if we live in the belief of "lucky breaks" as being the key to getting ahead, then the other side of the coin is that an unlucky break can lead to failure. We just can't have one without the other.

In the case of this man, his loss of job came about because of something a co-worker failed to do. The whole thing was regrettable and it appears that the man was unjustly treated. However, blaming the other person does not change the situation. Holding bitterness only poisons his system and impedes the flow of good into his life. How much better to hold to the ideal that "nothing can keep my own from me"? In a biblical story that you may remember from childhood, Joseph, after his brothers had sold him into slavery, said, "You may have intended it for evil, but God intended it for good." He picked up the pieces and went on to become Prime Minister of all Egypt.

Emerson wrote in "Compensation,"

The dice of God are always loaded. The world looks like a multiplication table or a mathematical equation, which, turn it how you will, balances itself. Take what figure you will, its exact value, no more nor less, still returns to you. Every secret is told, every crime is punished, every virtue rewarded, every wrong redressed, in silence and certainty. What we call retribution is the universal necessity by which the whole appears wherever a part appears.

Emerson really tells it as it is. You may want to read that again.

Carlyle said, "Genius is an uttering forth of the inspired soul of man." You may have thought of genius as a property of a unique and specially endowed individual. However, everyone of us has a uniqueness, which is our own particular genius. It is our own greater self, which has its own genius for good fortune. If crises threaten your security, don't hope for "good luck" or prate of misfortune, but let your genius for good fortune, the transcendent self within you, "utter forth" the word of confidence and courage. Hold on to an unfolding good that is most certainly yours.

When you discipline your mind to react to all changing circumstances with a projected positive thought, you bring into play your own genius for good fortune. Not only is it a radiating force that attracts good to you, it is also a catalyst that turns misfortune into good fortune. Lin Yutang, Chinese author and philologist, says, "Disappointment is like a medal. There is printing on both sides, and there is an advantage and disadvantage to what seems to be adversity." Through the mastery of your own inner self, you can turn the medal over and completely reverse all adversity. Your life becomes secure and predictable through your genius for good fortune.

61.   How to Get Rid of Your Crutches

There is an ancient truth that has found its way into many philosophies: *He Who Is Within Me Is Greater Than He Who Is in the World.* This means that you have the potential to meet and overcome any situation or experience that life may present you. You may have to work at it, to grow a little more, to dig a little deeper, to find the means of meeting and overcoming the need. But growth is what life is all about.

This is the one great and relevant thing that is overlooked in the midst of a host of irrelevancies in our education. Because we do not know it, we underestimate ourselves, and limit ourselves; we come too quickly to the conclusion that we are helplessly inadequate. Thus, we begin reaching for something or someone to buoy up our strength. If we could only know it, every time we reach for the leaning post we solidify the self-image of insufficiency and make the leaning post that much more of a crutch.

On the whole we are all too easy on ourselves. We give up too easily and thus we discover and use only a small part of our innate potential. I recall as a youth, when I was an aspiring trackman, how often I was tempted to drop out of distance races in the early part of the race, but I made the discovery that if I had my tussle with the temptation to quit, I could press past that point of fatigue and go on to new strength. I have found that this has its application in every experience in life.

Certainly we have ups and downs in all experiences. Man is not a machine. He has periods of varying energy. Nature, like a composer of music, intersperses rests. Knowing this, the self-disciplined person is neither discouraged nor baffled when results are not quickly evident. One who wants to succeed in the art of disciplined living—the art of self-reliance—must continue to strive no matter how discouraged. As American football coach Knute Rockne used to tell his players, "When the going gets tough, the tough get going." We should always go a little farther, beyond the point of fatigue, of weakness, of insufficiency. Don't reach for the crutch—go a little farther—keep on.

Of course if you want to get rid of crutches, you must be

willing to change your thinking. You can't rise to new strength while you are dwelling on your weaknesses. You can't be the strong person you are capable of becoming if you keep telling yourself what a weakling you are. Don't fall back on the convenient cliché, "But that's just the way I am." It is not really the way you are, it is only the degree to which you have been able to see the potentialities within you. But there is always more in you.

One of our problems is that our thoughts spring from external facts rather than from a consideration of what we possess within us. As long as this is the case we go on perpetuating the old circle of limitation. The remedy is to reverse the method of thinking and take the idea of your creative genius as the starting point. Begin with the idea that you are a whole creature with limitless potential through which to do and do well what needs to be done. Be a creative thinker and not just a reactor. In other words, don't wait to see what the day will bring. You bring to the day a positive state of mind and a happy expectation.

Ask yourself the question, "Do I really want to be free from my crutch, or do I simply think I should or think others think I should?" If you really do want to be free, then make a commitment to change your self-image. Weaknesses are habitual because your thought about yourself has been habitually negative. There is no such thing as inherent weakness. What is called "inherent weakness" is simply a subconscious idea of weakness that has become a bad mental habit. Begin now to make some new habits of thought.

Begin entertaining the possibility that you have the power in you to be more than you now are, the power to overcome, to stand alone, to be self-sufficient. Say, to yourself, "I can master this habit, and I will." But don't stop there. "I will" still deals with something to be done, and procrastination may still set in. "I will" deals with tomorrow. Get the here-and-now attitude. Say, "I can . . . I will . . . I am." In other words, always follow the "I can" and "I will" statements with the declaration "I am." This creates the identification with the process and accepts it in faith as already done. This is the Golden Key: see it in your mind and believe in your ability to realize it, and you will achieve it. Declare right now: "I can and I will overcome. . . . I am successful."

VII. The Art of Letting Go

62. Meet Mr. Rushmore

Did you ever stop to consider how the everyday events of our lives might appear if a camera were to record our ordinary activities and we could view them later on a screen? I am certain that most of us would give the impression that we are constantly being chased by something.

As an example, let us take a morning from the life of Mr. Rushmore. It is six o'clock in the morning. Mr. Rushmore's alarm gently reminds him that a new day has begun. And how does it begin? He drags himself out of bed with much groaning and sighing. Laboriously he goes through the routine of shaving and dressing. To his family's cheery "Good morning" he replies: "What's good about it?"

Breakfast is a quick affair, gulped down with one eye on the clock and the other on the morning paper. That finished, by way of farewell, he grunts, "Well, off to the salt mines," and hurries out the door. There's his bus rounding the corner. Watch Mr. Rushmore run! Obviously the driver is a fiend so the bus races away from him in a cloud of exhaust. Fuming, Rushmore returns for his car. "Who had the keys last?" he screams to his family. "You did, dear," his wife replies. Sure enough, there they are in his pocket.

Soon Mr. Rushmore is dodging in and out of traffic. Listen to the blasts of his automobile horn. One can almost make out the dire threats he mutters to other drivers who dare to impede his progress. And, of course, the lights are all against him. He gives the impression of a man out for track as he makes a dash for the elevator. Breathless, he arrives at his desk and notes with a rather dour smile of satisfaction that he has two minutes to spare. And thus, Mr. Rushmore establishes the tenor of his day. Small wonder his nerves are on edge, his stomach upset, and his head pounds and throbs before his workday has even begun.

Mr. Rushmore's case is, of course, terribly exaggerated. I would never act like that, nor would you. At least we wouldn't admit to it. But in our present hurry-scurry age, many of us work under great pressures, which cause us to do some rather peculiar things. When things are at their tensest peak, we often heave a sigh, and say, "Oh, if I could just get away from it all!"

That is exactly what you should do! I don't suggest you run off from your job or your responsibilities to sail away to Tahiti. That might help, but few of us can do that. And I rather suspect that Mr. Rushmore in Tahiti would still be Mr. Rushmore.

But I say again, we should get away from it all. The problem with most of us is that we live too close to the circumference of experience. We need, at least occasionally, to relax for a few minutes, and, as Tennyson put it, "labor for an inward stillness." There is within each of us a place of central calm in which we can find serenity, peace, and tranquility. I like Webster's definition for serene: "bright, clear, and calm; shining with clear, steady light. Placid, unruffled. Tranquil."

The next time you feel tense and hurried, acting like Mr. Rushmore, take a minute to "get away from it all." You might even use the definition of serenity as an affirmation. "I am bright, clear, and calm; I am shining with clear, steady light. I am placid and unruffled. I am tranquil." You will be amazed how such a practice can change your life.

63.   Twenty-Four Hours to Live

A great man was once asked, "If you knew that you had but six months to live, what would you do? How would you live?" Without a second thought he replied, "I would live one day at a time," proving that he was not only a great man, but he was a wise man too.

There is a story told of a philosophical clock that fell to meditating upon its future as it was put in its place for the first time. It reasoned that it had to tick twice each second, 120 times each minute, or 7200 times every hour—in twenty-four hours, 172,800 ticks. This meant 63,000,000 times each year. And in ten years it would have to tick 630,000,000 times! At this point the clock collapsed from nervous exhaustion. When finally it revived, it saw in a moment of insight that all it had to do was one tick at a time. And so it began, and now, after one hundred years, it is still a respected grandfather clock.

Sir William Osler, a Canadian doctor and one of the great men of medicine, used to suggest that *we live in day-tight compartments*. He said, "To do today's work well and not to bother about tomorrow is the secret of accomplishment. I owe whatever success I have had to this power of settling down to the day's work and trying to do it well to the best of my ability. So close the door upon yesterday and refuse to open the door leading to tomorrow. Life is important when it is lived in the Great Now."

Anyone can endure the challenges, the crises, the battles of just one day. It is only when we add the burdens of those two awful eternities—yesterday and tomorrow—that we break down. This is one of the principles by which Alcoholics Anonymous has been able to rescue thousands of hopeless men and women from the clutches of alcoholism. The individual can't endure the thought of giving up drink forever, but he *can* think of living one day, twenty-four hours, without a drink. Taking one day at a time, he veritably pulls himself up by the bootstraps.

But one doesn't need to be an alcoholic to profit from the idea of living one day at a time. You can overcome the tendency to indulge in grief and remorse over events of the past by realizing that yesterday, with its aches and pains, its cares and blunders, has passed forever from your control. You can walk confidently into the unknown of the future by giving all your attention to what you think, how you work, where you walk, today. There is a story of a traveler in ancient Greece who had lost his way. He asked directions of a man by the roadside, who turned out to be Socrates. "How can I reach Mt. Olympus?" the traveler asked. To this Socrates is said to have replied gravely, "Just make every step you take go in that direction."

Today is your day and mine. It is all there is or ever can be. Make today a wonderful day, the greatest day of your life, by walling it off from yesterday or tomorrow. Make every step you take today go in the direction of your dreams.

There is an old Sanskrit proverb that says, "Yesterday is but a dream and tomorrow is only a vision, but today well lived makes every yesterday a dream of happiness and every tomorrow a vision of hope. Look well therefore to this day."

64. A New Look at Tension

It is said that tension is the major problem of modern man living his hurried, harried life in a changing, uncertain world. This is the consensus of doctors, clinical psychologists, and ministers. All agree that we need to "relax and let go," to release our tensions and find an inner sense of peace.

Most of us do get too wrapped up in our work, too emotionally involved with our real or imagined problems, and too centered in ourselves and focused on our insufficiency and inferiority. But we are wrong if we think that we must be relieved of all tension. The physiologist talks about "body tone." This refers to "the normal degree of vigor and tension." To release all tension would actually cause a breakdown of the orderly functioning of the body.

Take a good look at your watch. You might say, in observing the tightly wound mainspring, "How tense it is! It should be relaxed and made free from tension." Yet if you release the tension of the mainspring, you stop the action of the watch. Much of what we call tension refers to the strain of working to accomplish difficult projects. We tell someone, "Why don't you relax and let go?" Yet if all the tension is taken from a person, if there is nothing for which one keeps working and striving, if there is nothing over which one gets wound up, one becomes like the watch with the relaxed mainspring, as alert as a bear in hibernation.

Popular psychology and "progressive religion" talk a lot about peace of mind. It is lauded as one of the major objectives in life. Now, in its positive form, peace of mind is a wonderful thing, and a most needful thing for every individual. However, it is likely that the term is misunderstood. It may lead to a peace-at-any-price sort of attitude that in turn can lead to complacency, indifference, and self-satisfaction.

Much that we call tension may be the result of resistance to problems and conditions because we feel unconsciously that life should be free from challenges of any kind. We tend to think that a challenging circumstance is a bad or negative thing, and that there surely must be something wrong with life or with our approach to life or it never would have come. We forget that often our greatest growth comes through our meeting the challenge of change, and that every problem has within it the potential of good for us. We may and certainly should meet life's crises at the expanse of our inner resources rather than at the expense of them.

Many of the bad effects of tension come from our awareness of the immensity of our tasks and our inadequacy in meeting them. Certainly we must change the thought of fear and worry, but this is no time to be lulled into complacency with the words "relax and let go." The need is to open our eyes to the infinite resources of the universe, and the will to believe that we can release our innate potential.

Abraham Lincoln said to his friends and neighbors on leaving home to accept the presidency of the United States, "Without the help of Him who attends me, I cannot succeed; with that help, I cannot fail." This is the way to quiet power. You may still need to work as hard as you ever did. You may still be faced with responsibilities that no one but you can shoulder. But you will not resist them or resent them or try to meet them with human resources alone.

65. The Need for Silence

In the biblical book of Ecclesiastes we find this wise observation: "To everything there is a season, and a time to every purpose under heaven . . . a time to keep silence, and a time to speak" (3:1–7, KJV). In our complex way of life today, though many of us pride ourselves on the way in which we order our lives, I wonder how many of us really find the time or make the time to keep silence?

Ann Morrow Lindbergh, in her delightful book *Gift from the Sea*, says,

The world today does not understand, in either man or woman, the need to be alone . . . Anything else will be accepted as a better excuse. If one sets aside time for a business appointment, a trip to the hairdresser, a social engagement, that time is accepted as inviolable. But if one says: I cannot come because that is my hour to be alone, one is considered rude, egotistical, or strange. What a commentary on our civilization, when being alone is considered suspect; when one has to apologize for it, make excuses, hide the fact that one practices it—like some secret vice!

I am wondering how many of us practice this "secret vice"? Pascal, the great French philosopher and mathematician said, "After observing humankind over a long period of years, I came to the conclusion that one of man's great troubles is his inability to be still." Every single one of us needs silence as much as nourishment. Not just the silence of sleep, but great islands of hush scattered through the day where we can pause and rest our eyes, our vocal cords, our ears, our minds, and our bodies.

There is no need to labor the point that most of us are surrounded by noise. The hammering of factories and the roar of traffic fill our ears from morning till night. Our systems become so accustomed to noise that we feel lonely and insecure when noises cease. Many a city dweller has reacted to a first night in the country with the thought "The quiet was so deafening that I couldn't sleep."

Many of our modern inventions and devices are designed to keep people from the "calamity" of being without sound entertainment. It is not uncommon to have a radio or television set in every room of a home, and they are often turned on as regularly as the light switch. An automobile without a radio is as old-fashioned as a horse and buggy. The advent of small portable radios and cassette players enables us to carry the din of raucous sound with us as we walk. And we have portable TV sets, too. A man may not know where he is going, but he can watch the early show or the late movie while he walks there.

One thing seems certain: this wall-to-wall and dawn-to-dusk sound will save us from the necessity of ever having to rub two thoughts together to make a luminous friction in our minds. It seems designed to save us from the awful vexation of thinking or of experiencing the horrible boredom of silence.

I have heard people complain that they never have any original ideas, that they never feel the flow of inspiration. I usually suggest, "Why not take time to get still and listen?" It is as impossible for people who surround themselves with activity and noise and ceaseless babble of conversation to experience the inflow of creative ideas as it is for pure water to flow through a pipe that is carrying crude oil.

If you want to be a more effective person, relaxed and free from tension, and if you want to experience original and creative ideas, remember the words from Ecclesiastes: "To everything there is a season . . . a time to keep silence, and a time to speak." Make time today for several periods of quiet reflection, meditation, or prayer.

66. Relax and Let Go

Relaxation is of vital importance to every one of us, and maintaining a relaxed mind and body is a full-time job. There is great vision in what the daughter of the hard-driving executive of a manufacturing concern had to say to her father in one of Clarence Buddington Kelland's novels:

"You like to have folks tense and grim all the time," she said. "I say what's the use. Take a man in the outfield. He can pick daisies or practice dance steps or jape with the bleachers nine-tenths of the game, so long as his eye is on the batter and he is under a fly ball when it gets belted his way. My idea—and I like it because it gives you time for fun—is to relax and enjoy yourself 'till the batter swats the ball."

One of America's outstanding efficiency experts used to say that we should use our moments of unavoidable delay for building up our energy reserves. Most of us take annual vacations. It is a good practice for everyone. But an annual vacation is not enough. We must learn how to take "minute" vacations, to master the art of the pause. What do you do when your car is halted at a red traffic light? Here is a perfect time to take a "minute" vacation. In the middle of a busy day of ceaseless activity, you may be slowed to a halt while the office boy delivers your copy to the boss for approval. Again, a perfect time to take a brief vacation. English poet George Herbert wrote: "When you are an anvil, hold you still; when you are a hammer, strike your fill."

Relaxation is an investment in new vigor, vitality and energy. It is a technique of opening the door so that new power may flow into our bodies, minds, and spirits. An elderly southern woman had the secret of letting go of bodily tensions. She said, "When ah works, ah works hard; but when ah sits, ah sits loose."

The strange thing is that often we try too hard to relax and the opposite result is achieved. Someone has suggested we imitate a person at rest—a kid lying on his back in the sun at the old swimming hole, or a man sitting in a boat fishing. In other words don't try to relax, just think about being lazy. A circus clown who has taken many sensational falls without being hurt says he tries to make his body as limp as an old rag doll. We can simulate this by holding the image of a restful person even while in the midst of a whirl of activity.

And, of course, we need to take time to relax the mind—to get still in a prayer-like solitude and to let great pools of quiet flow through our mind. We need to attune ourselves with the constructive forces of the universe, moving with life instead of trying to move counter to it. Instead of opposing people and circumstances we must learn to cooperate and harmonize. Instead of going around with chips on our shoulders, tense and ready for battle, we should relax and flow with the current of life, working with, and not against, each other.

Before this day is over, take a "minute" vacation. Relax the mind and the body. And make relaxation a daily habit. You'll live longer and better.

67. You Need Never Be Tired

One of the startling discoveries in the field of psychology is that no matter how hard you work, you do not need to get tired. The usual method of working wastes more energy than it uses. You can wear yourself out while sitting still waiting for a tardy friend. On the other hand, the heaviest kind of work can be done without fatigue, and done much better.

One important principle is that people can work much longer and harder if they have frequent brief rest periods—before they tire—instead of after. It is almost never your work that tires you but *how* you work.

Another important point is the need for relaxation. It is not usually muscular fatigue that is at the root of our exhaustion, but rather nervous fatigue, which may be measured by how easily little things "get on your nerves." The need is to get a sense of effortlessness into your work, to work with quiet, relaxed power. Since you have little voluntary control over your nerves, the problem resolves itself into the question of how to relax them. You do have voluntary control over your muscles, and by relaxing them you can relax your nerves through reflex action. You can't have a tantrum if your muscles refuse to kick and scream.

For example, go over your body frequently in your mind and ask yourself which muscles are too tense. Back muscles, shoulder muscles, neck muscles, even the frowning brow—wherever you find tensed muscles, relax them; they are wearing you out. Actually say to your eye muscles, "Relax, and let go!" to your legs, "Relax, and let go." This may seem like an odd thing to do, but try it. You will be amazed to learn that your words do have positive and creative influence over your whole system. You are really the master of this household that is your body.

A psychologist who kept some young men awake for six days and nights merely by keeping them interested concluded that what we call fatigue is often only boredom (this is what causes us to yawn). A sportsman may tramp for miles on a hunt, until his feet weigh tons; then up jumps the game, and presto! he is no longer tired but has called on reserves of emotional energy. It isn't just imagination—but real energy. When you are really interested, your ductless glands, the body's hypodermic needles, shoot you full of something even stronger than strychnine or arsenic.

You come home from work saying, "What a tough day at the office," stagger into your armchair, and think nothing could move you out of the house for any conceivable reason. And then the phone rings. It is Ed wanting to know if you would like to go bowling with the gang. You bound out of that chair with a new-found energy and off you go to enjoy a strenuous evening, returning home many hours later feeling fresh and relaxed. Again, you thought you were tired, but actually you were simply bored.

One of the great needs in life is the attitude by which we make play out of work. If you can find things that are interesting and exciting and fulfilling in the routine of your job, it will actually become like child's play. If you cannot do this, you will not draw upon your storehouse of powerful emotional energy. You will constantly feel tired before you *are* tired. And your work will be of poor quality. Stop feeling sorry for your poor overworked self. Take occasional rest periods during the day. Keep your muscles relaxed by ordering them to do so. And be alert to find ways to make your work more pleasant and more interesting. It will increase your energy, improve your work, and give your emotional energies a constructive outlet.

68. Sanctuary for You

Traveling in England a few years ago, I came across something that is reminiscent of a day long past. On the door of Durham Cathedral is a ponderous lion's head of bronze. It is the Sanctuary knocker. In medieval times, a fugitive could strike it on the stout oak doors and claim the ancient and holy right of sanctuary. He was not asked where he came from, nor what his situation was. He was required only to leave his weapons at the door and, sometimes, to remove his dust-covered garments and put on a special white robe of contemplation. Once within the sanctuary, he was safe from all pursuers. Not the famous Sheriff of Nottingham nor all the king's horses and all the king's men had power over him there.

Such sanctuaries are nonexistent now, in fact there is no sanctuary from the far more insidious and hurtful attacks to which we are exposed today. The atmosphere is heavy with impalpable fears, and we are harassed by oppressive shadows of sorrow and insecurity. From dawn to dusk we are exposed to noise: the telephone and doorbell, the boy next door practicing his piano, the barking of the dog across the street, the screech of tires and honking of horns, the rumbling of buses and the clatter of garbage cans. We are so conditioned to noise that it almost becomes necessary to our comfort. Some people actually cannot "rest" without the accustomed noises.

How great is our need for silence, for sanctuary! Seeking sanctuary does not mean running away from reality; it merely means turning our backs for a few moments upon the torturous, self-made problems that daily exhaust our fortitude. Seeking sanctuary is, if anything, a turning *to* reality—a reality that we seldom see or feel in the midst of distractions of our day. It means attaining peace and guidance within ourselves. A few moments of silence, of quiet relaxation and contemplation, in the midst of a busy day will work wonders for anyone.

I know an extremely successful businessman who takes such a period every working day of his life. It is an office ritual: at ten o'clock in the morning, when the work has piled high and the tensions are at their peak, he closes his door. If he is in the midst of a consultation with someone he interrupts the meeting and says it is time for his silent period; he invites them to join him or wait in the outer office. He jokingly says it wouldn't matter if he were sitting with the President of the United States; he would not fail to observe this moment of solitude. And even as he says it we know he is not joking. At precisely ten o'clock he sits back in his chair, closes his eyes, and lets great pools of silence drift through his mind. He says this ten minutes a day has been the real key to his success.

How does this ritual of self-communion recharge the jaded batteries of the soul? Well, each of us has within a secret of energy, too seldom tapped, too often undiscovered. We find it as we let go and let that which is greater than ourselves flow in us and through us.

Sanctuary does not depend upon lighted candles, organ music, or stained glass (though some people find such an environment a great help in contemplation). It is not a question of theology or dogma. It is a simple practice of an inner relationship basic to every one of us, which most religions articulate. Wherever you are, whatever your need may be, there is silence for you, there is sanctuary for you—right where you are.

69. Tranquility for You

It is not easy to keep calm and unruffled in the complex context of modern living. But, on the other hand, hitting the ceiling is no way to get up in the world! If you have been under tension and stress in your work, or if conflicts in human relations have kept you under the influence of slow-burning anger, frustration, and irritation; if you have been pushing the panic button too soon and too often, you can find poise and tranquility without aspirin or tranquillizers. You can learn to live with a relaxed and confident spirit.

The great teachers and philosophers of the ages have agreed on one thing: that life is lived from inside out; that it doesn't really matter what happens around you or to you. The only thing that really counts is what happens *in* you. You can't control the world or the people in it, but you can control the thoughts you entertain about them. In the world of your mind, you are king—or you can be. No matter what demands may be made upon you or what crises you may face, just as there is a place of calm at the center of the hurricane, there is also within you a dynamic center of poise and power that is always equal to life, but we must relate to it and turn it on.

This takes practice, of course, but it can be done. You are living in an intelligent universe and something of that intelligence is within you. There is an infinite creative process at the root of all things, and it is working in you. Your desire to experience poise and tranquility in the face of things is your reassurance that you can achieve it, if you just mobilize the faith to believe that you can. Get the thought into your mind that there is a place of peace within you; that this is *your* peace. Declare for yourself: "I believe that I am peaceful at heart, and that I can let this inner peace sweep over my mind, body, and affairs."

Now as I paint a word picture of your life as you secretly desire it, let your mind visualize it as being real, and believe it as being you:

You are now centered in the dynamic spirit of tranquility. You are serene and undisturbed as you think of your life and affairs. You are undisturbed by doubt and fear. You now feel the quiet surge of peace and power through you, and your faith grows.

Wherever you are, at home or abroad, working or playing, the serenity of your spirit brings peace and harmony to your environment. Your days are uncrowded because you do not waste energy and time in worrying. You are free from all sense of being overburdened or unappreciated. You are not irritated by weather, mistakes, or interruptions, for your emotions are attuned to the refreshing, healing, and harmonizing spirit of tranquility.

You are established in complete control of mind and body. Loving and peaceable at heart, you radiate harmony, strength, and courage to the world. A newly awakened joy brightens your countenance, colors your thoughts and words, and lends grace to your deeds and decisions. Your tranquil spirit protects the nerves and organs of your body from unnecessary wear and tear and you abound in health.

You have a sense of right perspective, so that you do not minimize great needs nor make mountains out of molehills. You quietly realize that you *can* do what you need to do. The quiet power and mastery of your true inner self frees you from all uncertainty, confusion, and unrest.

Each hour of the day yields its full quota of strength, joy, and contentment to you. You are now centered in the dynamic spirit of tranquility, and you are refreshed, renewed, and at peace with life and with the world.

70.   Slow Down and Catch Up

We are living in an age of speed—in a time when we can travel long distances in short periods and do tasks in a fraction of the time it once required because of the new technology. But the question we must ask from time to time is, What do we do when we arrive at that distant place we traveled to at such a frantic pace? What do we do with the time we save with our labor-saving devices? Why make the frantic trips if we fail to experience the joy of traveling? Or as American poet Edwin Markham puts it, "Why build these cities glorious, if man unbuilded goes?"

We often find ourself like the White Rabbit in Lewis Carroll's *Alice in Wonderland*, running about crying, "I'm late, I'm late, I'm late." But the problem is, we aren't really late, we are out of tune with the larger meaning of life. We are straining for accomplishment at the expense of our souls. We need to slow down and let the soul catch up. Slow down—stop frantically trying to *find* life, and get caught up in *living* life.

Much of our hurry comes from a secret fear that "it's later than you think," that life is a journey between certain limited points and we must hurry along to cram everything we can into the journey, that "life is all too short." But this is a false belief. Time does not come into existence moment by moment, second by second, and then pass on to nothingness. Time is the creation of human consciousness. There is no ticking clock in the universe, and there can be no shortage of time in human experience. When we hurry, we trap ourselves in a false idea of time. The clock and calendar become our masters; we march or run obediently. Get off this false treadmill. Slow down and get really caught up with the true unfoldment of life.

Whenever you are late, or think you are burdened with urgency, something has gotten out of tune. Rushing will not re-establish that attunement any more than racing your engine will get your car back into gear when it has slipped out. The need is to pause, take a break, take a time of quiet reflection on the allness of eternity in which you live, and watch the feelings of rush and hurry and the related fear slip right out of mind.

You may have been conditioned by the philosophy of industriousness and ingenuity, which sets forth the theme: *Do it now!* Undoubtedly there are those who need some discipline in order to activate themselves and break out of their inertial patterns of lethargy and procrastination. But the greater problem is the attitude that we must always get and keep busy. Robert Louis Stevenson once said, "Extreme busyness is a symbol of deficient vitality," inferring that the bursting display of energy might well camouflage a large spiritual vacuum. There are times we feel compelled to "do it now" when it might be wiser to do it tomorrow instead. Sometimes the most urgent need in the midst of the feeling of urgency is to pause and relax—to slow down and catch up. Often rush and urgency become such a habit that we can not really tell whether we are rushing because we feel things are urgent or whether we feel things are urgent because of the habit of rushing.

Check up on yourself when you begin a task. Are you relaxed and confident, or anxious and rushed? If the latter is the case, you will just waste a lot of time and effort until you get caught up. Lay it aside for a while and take a walk until you can get yourself caught up in poise and confidence. It has been said that "leisure is the occasion and the capacity for steeping oneself in the whole of creation." There is a part of you that is transcendent to time, and you can experience it in quiet meditation. When you catch that inward feeling of timelessness, then you can do your task in "no time at all"—in a sense you do it not in time but in eternity. Get this idea into your consciousness and you will come to live and work in the world of time, but you will have your being centered in eternity.

71. The Art of Sleeping

If you have been having trouble sleeping at night, here is a thought that can change all that. You can learn to relax and let go of all the tensions and pressures built up through your day, and to drop off, like a baby, into a restful and refreshing sleep. Perhaps you have had times when you have worried through the night over a problem of some sort. Has it never occurred to you that worry is not a reflex action? The problem doesn't cause the worry. You have engaged in worry because this is precisely the way you have determined to meet your situation. Startling as it may sound, you sleep when you make up your mind that you want to sleep more than you want to worry.

Most of us carry a little psychological knapsack on our backs into which we toss the problems of the day as it progresses. But a knapsack makes a mighty poor pillow. Thus, on retiring at night it is important to lay aside consciously the accumulation of burdens and to empty the mind of fear, bitterness, enmity, and the chronic sense of responsibility, much in the same way as we empty our pockets and lay aside our garments. The expression "let's sleep on it" is too often taken literally, while it actually means to forego a decision until we have had a night's rest.

Napoleon, for all his faults, was a master of mental discipline. He thought of his mind as a chest of drawers into which he put ideas. He turned from one subject to another by closing one drawer and opening another. He was never kept awake by worry, for if he wanted to sleep, he simply shut all the drawers, and sleep came instantly.

Most people have so conditioned their minds to identify their beds as the place to plan work for the next day, to go over the problems of the past, and to indulge in self-pity, that they tend to dread going to bed at all. These people will often sleep on the subway, at their desks, or in front of TV, but as soon as their heads hit the pillow, they are wide awake. We need to make a conscious attempt to identify bed with sleep; to make a covenant that the bed is off-limits to negative thoughts. The bed is a sanctuary of rest and relaxation and sleep.

We need to take time and put our affairs in order before retiring. A farm handyman said his chief asset was being able to sleep when the wind blew. At first this puzzled the farmer, but he later discovered that this meant the man always took care of things so that there was no need for concern in a storm. If we leave loose ends in our affairs and in our unresolved thoughts about them, crises catch us unprepared. I like the words quoted by King George of England during World War II: "I said to a man at the gate of the year, 'Give me a light so that I can tread safely into the unknown.' And he said to me, 'Go out into the darkness and put your hand into the hand of God . . . It shall be to you better than light, and safer than a known way.'"

A technique that has been extremely helpful to many is the process of suggesting relaxation to the various muscles of the body. One man refers to it as "putting the family to bed." You are the master of your mind and body, so you simply talk to the muscles of the body, quietly and firmly telling them to relax and let go. You can make it an exercise-beginning with the top of the head, down through the areas of tension (eyes, throat, shoulders, heart, stomach, hips, legs) right down to the bottom of your feet. Just say to each part, each muscle: "relax and let go." You will fall asleep before you get the family tucked in for the night. But don't worry about that—the magic is not in any special process, though certainly the power of your suggestion is extremely influential. The important thing is that while you are consciously thinking about relaxing the body, you are not thinking about your concerns. Try this technique, preceded, of course, by a new identification of your bed as a place of sleep, and by the act of laying aside your psychological knapsack, and, as a wise man once said, "sleep will be a gentle maid, as beautiful as an angel, who brings her lovely wares for the one who rests without fear or anxiety, safe in her everlasting arms."

72.   Freedom and Solitude

This is an age of tests and quizzes. We love to test ourselves, to check up on ourselves. Newspapers and magazines are full of these self-testing quizzes, though most of them are so incomplete as to serve little purpose other than giving us the opportunity to salve our vanity.

Here is a little test that will tell volumes about you: What do you do with your leisure time? What are your requirements for a vacation? What do you do when freed from a busy life, a busy schedule of challenging problems, when life affords you an infrequent period during which you have nothing to do? What would be your reaction to a suggestion that you spend one hour in a room by yourself with no radio or TV, no books, no newspapers, nothing but a chair? Your answer reveals much about your nature that you may not know yourself.

The life of every man requires silence, solitude, rest, and relaxation. These periods of quiet, "cushions of silence," are the shock absorbers of life. Perhaps the reason so many of us fear solitude is that we have not really come to know ourselves. We live superficial lives at the circumference of our being. We enter our home and immediately flip on the radio or TV regardless of what it might be offering. We get bored with what is on, and the silence of the room is deafening. We pace the floor, then try to lose ourselves in a book. Finally we give up and bury our head in a pillow.

One of the great needs of our time is the art of getting to know ourselves, of getting along with ourselves, and learning to enjoy our own company. It is doubtful that we can ever get along with other individuals or other nations until we do. I wonder sometimes if we can ever really get along with *ourselves* until we learn to get along without so many of the things we think are necessities of life. It is a curious phenomenon that we can get people to die for the liberty of the world who will not make the little sacrifices that are needed to free themselves from their own personal bondage.

Go out and look around in any department store and you will be amazed at how many things you can see that we like to think are necessities of life, things that our grandfathers got along perfectly well without. None of them were included in the lives of the ancient Greeks, who gave birth to more great men than any similar period of history has been able to produce.

Every once in a while I like to take out Thoreau's *Walden* and read it over again. It is completely impractical and idealistic and foolhardy, but it is a good tonic. Thoreau was a Harvard graduate who built a hut for himself on the shores of a little lake near Concord, Massachusetts, and lived in it for two years and two months. He threw worry out of the window, reduced his living expenses to a point he could provide for them with the labor of a very small part of his days, and so freed the remainder of his life for reading and writing and tramps through the woods.

We can't all do what Thoreau did, and I do not suggest that anyone try it today, but we can learn something about what he was driving at. We have created for ourselves a society with so many luxurious necessities that we actually spend a large part of our time and our money, vast portions of our life itself, in working for certain things we could easily do without; things we have little time to enjoy because we are too busy working for them and paying for them and repairing and maintaining them.

I do not suggest that we go back to pioneer days, that we all return to the country, though it might do us all a world of good to do so occasionally. But I do think that we owe it to ourselves to bring something of the solitude and simplicity of former times along with us today. It is imperative if we are going to remain spiritually and mentally healthy and creative.

73. From Fretting to Letting

Many people make life unnecessarily difficult for themselves by dissipating power and energy through fuming and fretting. The word "fume" means to boil up, to blow off, to seethe. The word "fret" is equally descriptive. It is the noise of a sick child in the night, a petulant half-cry half-whine. To fret is definitely a childish action, yet it vividly describes the emotional reaction of many adults.

Several thousand years ago a shepherd poet wrote, "Fret not thyself." This is far more appropriate advice in our day of hurried, harried living. We need to stop fuming and fretting and become peaceful if we are to live more effectively and, some doctors might add, if we are going to go on living at all. Good advice, but how do we go about following it?

One way is to reduce the tempo of our pace. Many of us simply do not realize how accelerated the rate of our life has become, or the speed and stress and tension with which we are driving ourselves. We suffer from overstimulation and super-excitement. This produces both physical and mental illness, fatigue, and a sense of frustration, so that we fume and fret about everything from our personal troubles to the state of the nation.

How do we reduce our pace? One way is to take time to reflect upon the rhythm of the universe, the changing of the seasons, the silent sweep of the stars. It helps to take a few minutes during the day to relax and look out the window or look out of the maze of our vital concerns. The "coffee break" has become as much a part of our business day as the lunch hour. It is supposed to be a period of rest and recreation. But I sometimes wonder how much actual *re*creating is done during this period, especially after hearing the tone of discussions. It may be that a meditation break or prayer break would be more effective. We must find a way to stop fretting and start letting the creative forces of the universe find expression in us and through us in a quiet and easy power.

A physician I know of gave some whimsical but effective advice to a patient. The man, an aggressive, go-getter type, had told the doctor what an enormous load he was carrying, and how much depended on him. He said he had to take work home every night because he alone could do it right. The doctor wrote a prescription, and this is what it said: "Take one hour off every working day and go for a long walk, and take half a day off each week and spend it in a cemetery."

In astonishment the patient demanded, "Why should I spend half a day in a cemetery?" "Because," answered the doctor, "I want you to wander around and look at the gravestones of men who got there because they thought, as you do, that the whole world rested on their shoulders. I suggest that you sit on one of the tombstones and ask some challenging questions of yourself concerning why your life is so hectic, and don't leave until you find some satisfying answers." Well, the patient got the idea. He slowed his pace. He learned to delegate authority. He stopped fuming and fretting, and began to really let go and let things work instead of feeling that he had to make them work. He got peaceful with himself and the rest of the world. And he now does better work and is developing a more competent organization.

The next time you find yourself anxious and tense about your work or about anything that concerns you, stop fretting and start letting. Relax and let the forces within and around you work with and for you.